Legal Guidebook for Closely Held Corporations

SECOND EDITION

CORPORATE LAWS COMMITTEE

AMERICAN BAR ASSOCIATION
Business Law Section

Cover design by Catherine Zaccarine.

Printed in the United States of America.

27 26 25 24 23   5 4 3 2 1

ISBN: 978-1-63905-367-4

Discounts are available for books ordered in bulk. Special consideration is given to state bars, CLE programs, and other bar-related organizations. Inquire at Book Publishing, ABA Publishing, American Bar Association, 321 N. Clark Street, Chicago, Illinois 60654-7598.

www.shopABA.org

Contents

Preface

This *Guidebook*, prepared by the Corporate Laws Committee of the Business Law Section of the American Bar Association, provides a concise, practical overview of important legal principles that govern directors, officers, and shareholders of closely held corporations. Unless specifically provided to the contrary, the terminology and legal rules discussed in this *Guidebook* conform to the Model Business Corporation Act (the "Model Act") without discussing individual differences between states. Among the state corporation statutes, there are three general groupings: (1) the Model Act, which provides the basis for the corporation laws of about two-thirds of the states; (2) Delaware, which has its own template (and a couple of smaller states follow it) and the most recognizable in corporate law because a majority of public corporations have chosen to incorporate there; and (3) some of the larger states, such as California and New York, which have their own templates, distinctive from either the Model Act or Delaware. Readers should be aware that the state statute applicable to their corporation may differ from the Model Act. When faced with a specific issue, directors, officers, shareholders, and their legal counsel should examine the particular state statute of the corporation's state of incorporation.

This *Guidebook* replaces *Managing Closely Held Corporations: A Legal Guidebook*, which was published in 2003. Given the time lapse, this new edition required a thorough update and it was necessary to add new topics that have emerged in the last two decades. The Committee is grateful to the members who worked on this first edition.

This *Guidebook* is different from other available sources in a number of ways:

- **It deals with the special concerns and challenges involved in closely held corporations—those with relatively few shareholders and no public trading market for their equity securities.** The corporation's distinctive attributes and detailed statutory operating rules have made it the most used entity in modern society, attractive across a broad spectrum of businesses. While there is significant diversity in the types and sizes of businesses operating as closely held corporations, many of the legal issues facing directors, officers, and shareholders are the same, from the smallest closely held corporation operating at a local or even neighborhood level to the largest operating around the globe.

- **It covers legal concerns of directors, officers, and shareholders.** In publicly held corporations, most shareholders are passive investors with little connection to, or control over, management and little occasion to deal directly with the corporation. There may be little or no overlap between the decision-makers (management) and the risk-takers (shareholders). In closely held corporations, on the other hand, much greater congruency of decision-making and risk-taking exists. Most of the directors and officers are also significant shareholders. Consequently, a guidebook addressing closely held corporations needs to address all three roles.
- **It focuses on the law of corporate governance—the legal rules relating to the respective powers and duties of directors, officers, and shareholders.** This *Guidebook* does not purport to summarize all the various bodies of law relevant to closely held businesses. It focuses instead on crucial, common-denominator corporate law issues relating to structure, management, and decision-making. Who has the power to approve which corporate actions? How are those actions taken? What duties of care, loyalty, good faith, fairness, or disclosure do directors, officers, and shareholders owe to the corporation and each other? What liabilities may result from breaching those duties?

Chapter 1 (*Basic Concepts*) outlines some of the most basic and important concepts involved in the closely held corporate form and the important characteristics of a closely held corporation that are fundamentally different from the publicly held business that often defines the general thinking about a corporation.

Chapter 2 (*The Structure of Corporate Action*) discusses the articles of incorporation and bylaws of the corporation; the traditional roles of directors, officers, and shareholders; and how the board of directors and shareholders can take action. The chapter also describes the default rules of corporate governance provided in the Model Act and most state corporation statutes, as well as the provisions of the Model Act and state corporation statutes that allow flexibility for closely held corporations to modify those default rules to fit the needs of their participants. (Chapters 5 and 6 discuss how shareholders can accomplish this in multiple settings.)

Chapter 3 (*Director, Officer, and Shareholder Duties and Rights*) discusses the responsibilities and duties applicable to directors, including when conflicts of interest arise or in the case of a merger, other extraordinary transaction or when the corporation is in distress, as well as the responsibilities and duties applicable to officers. In addition, the chapter describes the duties of shareholders or affiliated groups of shareholders that control the corporation.

Chapter 4 (*Shareholder Remedies*) addresses possible minority shareholder remedies in the context of oppression by the majority shareholder. The chapter describes two kinds of state-provided legal remedies: corporation statutes providing minority shareholders liquidity options when there has been majority oppression; and common law remedies based on case law, including breach of duties owed to minority shareholders. The chapter also briefly sets out the intersection between contracting and state-provided remedies, then details the specifics of remedies provided by statute such as direct and derivative litigation, and concludes with other remedies such as appraisal and alternative dispute resolution processes.

Chapter 5 (*Modifying Traditional Board and Shareholder Roles and Default Corporate Structures*) describes the use of particular provisions in the articles of incorporation, bylaws, and shareholder agreements to alter the statutory default rules for corporate governance. The chapter explores the various modifications that may be available to a closely held corporation by specific examination of those allowed by the Model Act. This includes the use of multiple classes of stock, preemptive rights, and Model Act § 7.32, which allows for private unanimous agreements among the shareholders to accomplish specific matters that may be inconsistent with one or more default provisions of the Model Act.

Chapter 6 (*Buy–Sell Agreements and Other Restrictions on Stock Transfers*) focuses on the use of contracts to address the ownership and transfer of shares. The chapter discusses buy–sell agreements and restricting the transfer of shares, each of which can be important in the planning process to ensure control, voting, and ownership of the corporation's shares address the respective goals and objectives of the shareholders in a closely held corporation over time.

Chapter 7 (*Raising Money, Issuing Shares, and Distributing Assets*) discusses financing a corporation, distributions to shareholders such as dividends and stock redemptions, and ownership interests for employees.

Chapter 8 (*Merger, Sale of Assets, and Change of Entity*) discusses mergers, asset sales, and entity changes. Mergers and asset sales can be used to recapitalize a corporation, create a holding company structure, or acquire other entities. A corporation may change its form of entity by converting from a corporation into a different legal entity, such as a limited liability company (LLC), and may also change its state of incorporation from one state to another through a domestication.

Chapter 9 (*Director, Officer, and Shareholder Liability Concerns*) discusses limitations of director liability, indemnification provisions for directors and officers, and piercing the corporate veil.

Chapter 10 (*Corporate Books, Records, and Reporting*) describes corporate record-keeping requirements and discusses directors' rights with respect to a corporation's books and records, how such rights can be limited or restricted when the director has a conflict of interest, and shareholder information rights and requests.

A number of the concepts discussed in this *Guidebook* have close analogs with other forms of organization, such as partnerships and LLCs. Choice of entity is an important decision for those organizing a closely held business that involves a complex balancing of tax and other important considerations. Organizers of a closely held business need expert advice to make an informed choice. This *Guidebook*, however, takes choice of the corporate form as a given. The characteristics of noncorporate forms of organization and the considerations involved in choice of entity are beyond the scope of this *Guidebook*.

Corporate Laws Committee

The Corporate Laws Committee of the Section of Business Law of the American Bar Association is composed of active or former practicing lawyers, law professors, regulators, and judges with corporate expertise. In addition to this *Guidebook*, the Committee is responsible for the publication of the *Corporate Director's Guidebook* and other scholarly writings and the development of the *Model Business Corporation Act* (the *Model Act*).

The *Model Act*, first issued in 1950, has been adopted substantially in its entirety by 36 states and other jurisdictions. In addition, important provisions have been adopted by many other states. The *Model Act* has played an important role in the development of corporate law in the United States and elsewhere.

The Committee serves as the standing editorial board for the *Model Act*, reviewing, revising, and updating its provisions on a continuing basis. Moreover, the Committee publishes the *Model Business Corporation Act Annotated*, a comprehensive compilation of the *Model Act* with cases and authorities relevant to its provisions.

The roster of active Committee participants during the publication of this *Guidebook* (including appointed members, senior advisors, reporters, secretaries, consultants, and liaisons from other ABA committees) is listed below.

Claudia H. Allen
Chicago, IL

Beth E. Berg
Chicago, IL

C. Stephen Bigler
Wilmington, DE

Willard L. Boyd III
Des Moines, IA

C. Kent Carlson
Seattle, WA

Mary Ann Carlson
Bratenahl, OH

Douglas K. Chia
Princeton, NJ

Nathaniel L. Doliner
Tampa, FL

Robert W. Downes
New York, NY

Michelle Adams Earley
Austin, TX

Karl John Ege
Seattle, WA

Patricia Enerio
Wilmington, DE

Andrea M. Farley
Atlanta, GA

Margaret M. Foran
Newark, NJ

Mark J. Gentile
Wilmington, DE

Maureen Brennan Gershanik
New Orleans, LA

Keir Gumbs
Washington, DC

Steven M. Haas
Richmond, VA

James J. Hanks, Jr.
Baltimore, Maryland

Carol Hansell
Toronto, ON

Keith F. Higgins
Boston, MA

James D. Honaker
Wilmington, DE

Michele D. Johnson
Orange County, CA

William D. Johnston
Wilmington, DE

Igor Kirman
New York, NY

John H. Lawrence, Jr.
Hartford, CT

Jonathan C. Lipson
Philadelphia, PA

Scott E. Ludwig
Huntsville, AL

David B. H. Martin
Washington, DC

David C. McBride
Wilmington, DE

Sue Meng
New York, NY

John F. Olson
Washington, DC

Sarah Payne
Palo Alto, CA

Elizabeth Pollman
Philadelphia, PA

Thomas E. Rutledge
Louisville, KY

Hillary A. Sale
Washington, DC

Philip Schwartz
Fort Lauderdale, FL

Larry P. Scriggins
Great Cacapon, WV

The Honorable Collins J. Seitz, Jr.
Wilmington, DE

John A. Seethoff
Redmond, WA

Megan Wischmeier Shaner
Norman, OK

David M. Silk
New York, NY

Laurie A. Smiley
New Orleans, LA

A. Gilchrist Sparks, III
Wilmington, DE

Robert B. Thompson
Washington, DC

The Honorable E. Norman Veasey
Wilmington, DE

Patricia O. Vella
Wilmington, DE

Leigh Walton
Nashville, TN

Kristine M. Wellman
Wilmington, DE

R. Daniel Witschey, Jr.
Houston, TX

John Mark Zeberkiewicz
Wilmington, DE

CHAPTER

1 Basic Concepts

This chapter explains a few basic legal concepts that all directors, officers, and shareholders of closely held corporations must understand, each of which is described in more detail throughout this *Guidebook*.

A. CORPORATION, ARTICLES OF INCORPORATION, AND BYLAWS

A corporation is an entity separate from its directors, officers, and shareholders, having the legal attributes provided in the state corporation statute under which it is created. Unlike the sole proprietorship and general partnership forms of business organization, a corporation comes into being only if specific acts are taken: articles of incorporation (known in some states, including Delaware, as a certificate of incorporation) containing required provisions must be filed with the appropriate government office (normally the secretary of state) in the state of incorporation, and a fee must be paid. Once the corporation is properly formed, it will continue in existence until it is dissolved. In addition to being the "birth certificate" of the corporation, the articles of incorporation also serve as a basic public record of legally required information about the corporation.

The bylaws are a set of more detailed rules of corporate governance that are required by most corporation statutes. Corporate bylaws usually lay out rules for shareholder and board meetings (e.g., when, where, and who may call; notice; quorum; and voting requirements), officer titles and duties, indemnification of directors and officers, and other important matters. Unlike the articles of incorporation, the bylaws are not required to be filed with the state and are a private document typically kept with other corporate records, including in the minute book.

B. DIRECTORS, OFFICERS, AND SHAREHOLDERS

Shareholders (or stockholders in a number of states, including Delaware) are the owners of the corporation. Unlike partners in a general partnership (who participate equally in the management of the partnership business unless agreed to the contrary), shareholders of a corporation are, by law, given the right to vote on certain enumerated items of corporate business: election of directors, amendments to the articles of incorporation and bylaws, and certain fundamental transactions (mergers, statutory share exchanges, major sales of corporate assets, and dissolution).

Directors are elected by the shareholders. The board of directors has nearly unilateral authority to approve all other corporate actions. The Model Act and most state corporation statutes permit shareholders to vary this vesting of residual authority in the board of directors (and even to dispense with the board of directors altogether) through a shareholder agreement. Shareholders in closely held corporations frequently customize voting control to ensure desired board composition or balance of power on key corporate actions through use of multiple classes of stock with differing voting rights, shareholder agreements, voting agreements, or voting trust arrangements. See Chapter 5 for a discussion of these types of agreements and arrangements.

Officers of the corporation are elected by the board of directors and have the authority and responsibilities delegated to them either in the bylaws or by specific board resolutions. Officers may also have implied authority by virtue of their positions, at least with respect to ordinary business transactions. The Model Act and most state corporation statutes permit the board great latitude in deciding what officers the corporation should have and what their titles, duties, and responsibility should be. The Model Act and most state corporation statutes permit one person to serve more than one, or even all, officer functions; however, some state corporation statutes require certain officer functions to be named.

C. THE CLOSELY HELD CORPORATION

A closely held corporation is commonly a corporation that has a relatively small number of shareholders and no active trading market for its securities. The term is frequently used to refer to any corporation that is not a publicly held corporation. A publicly held corporation has an organized, separate trading market for its equity securities and may have thousands of shareholders. Closely held corporations include a very diverse range of business associations from one-shareholder corporations to family-owned businesses to wholly owned subsidiaries to corporate joint ventures. Although a closely held corporation may be a small business, closely held status has nothing to do with size. A number of the largest corporations in the world, in terms of assets and revenues, are closely held.

Although closely held corporations come in many types and sizes, they share common attributes. These attributes include the following:

1. Shareholders Frequently Are Also Directors and Officers

In publicly held corporations, most shareholders are passive investors with little connection to, or control over, management and little occasion to deal directly with the corporation. In closely held corporations, on the other hand, directors and officers are generally also significant shareholders and active participants in the day-to-day business of the corporation who generally all know each other. Some important consequences flow from this attribute.

- **Who becomes a shareholder is important.** Shareholders in closely held corporations generally want to control transfers of equity securities so that unwanted outsiders do not become participants in the business. This is usually done through contractual restrictions on transfer of shares. See Chapter 6 for a discussion of buy–sell agreements.
- **Conflicts of interest may be frequent.** The overlapping roles of shareholders and of directors and officers mean that a transaction involving the corporation frequently involves a conflict between the interests of a shareholder and of a director or officer and those of the corporation. These conflict of interest transactions pose special problems for the board of directors. See Chapters 3 and 9 for a discussion of these conflict of interest issues.
- **Difficulty of multiple roles.** When a shareholder serves as a director or officer, the self-interest of the shareholder may conflict with the interests of the other shareholders or the corporation as a whole. Even though a shareholder is free to vote and otherwise act in their own interest, a director or officer owes loyalty to the corporation. A shareholder who serves as director or officer must remember that each of those roles will have certain duties and responsibilities to the corporation. See Chapter 3 for a further discussion of the director's and officer's duty of loyalty in conflict of interest situations. The officer of a corporation who serves as a director also has a dual role. In matters involving compensation or other employment

arrangements, the officer may have a personal interest that conflicts with the interests of the corporation. As employees, officers also have heightened duties to the corporation that differ from the supervisory duties of directors. See Chapter 3 for a discussion of the duties of officers. Customers, suppliers, bankers, lawyers, and other people with relationships to the corporation may be asked to become directors. Inherent conflicts of interest may exist when a person with a business relationship with the corporation serves as a director. A lawyer for the corporation who also serves as a director faces special concerns.

2. Management Structure and Corporate Governance Rules May Be Customized

Management structure and corporate governance rules are frequently customized in closely held corporations because some of the default corporate law rules will not work for participants in the closely held setting. Customization is accomplished through the use of provisions in the articles of incorporation or bylaws, shareholder agreements, multiple classes of stock with differing voting rights, voting agreements, or voting trust arrangements. These arrangements may be used to ensure desired board composition or desired balance of power on decisions regarding key corporate actions. Shareholders forming a closely held corporation often have preconceived expectations regarding structure and governance that do not conform to the basic default rules under the relevant state corporation statute (e.g., a desire that all shareholders must be directors or must approve expenditures over a certain limit). Various techniques can be used to customize structure and governance to meet these expectations. Using these techniques to ensure expectations are met is an important part of the planning and organization for closely held corporations, especially where investors include factions or constituencies (e.g., branches of a family or venture capital investors) whose self-interests may diverge. Directors of closely held corporations involving such customized balancing will want to learn to operate within the customized rules the corporation adopts and must be ready to deal with difficult cross-allegiances and conflicts that may arise when directors attempt to represent the interests of one faction or constituency at the same time as fulfilling their duties to the corporation and to all shareholders.

3. Investment in a Closely Held Corporation May Have Little Liquidity

Because a closely held corporation has no active trading market for its shares, a shareholder who wants to sell shares in the corporation may have little ability to find a buyer. And, even if a buyer is found, sales of stock frequently must be made at a discount to value as a proportionate share of the business. Shareholders who have a falling out with other shareholders in a closely held corporation may find that the only market for their shares consists of those other shareholders with whom they are at odds. The economic pressure on an outcast shareholder in a closely held corporation may be even greater if the outcast's primary income is derived as an employee of the corporation.

- **Buy–sell agreements are substitutes for market liquidity.** Liquidity concerns of individual shareholders, as well as concerns of all shareholders regarding who can invest with them, can be at least partially addressed by putting contractual buy–sell mechanisms in place at the outset. Consideration of such agreements is an important part of corporate planning and organization and can help reduce the risk of hardship and disputes. Buy–sell arrangements can provide for the redemption of shares by the corporation or purchase of shares by other shareholders upon changes in circumstances, such as death, disability, or termination of employment. See chapter 6 for a discussion of the types of provisions found in buy–sell agreements.
- **Buy–sell agreements are no guarantee against disputes, litigation, and liability.** Even well-conceived buy–sell agreements may not anticipate all problems arising from a falling out among shareholders. Courts in some jurisdictions have not viewed themselves as constrained by the terms of buy–sell agreements in fashioning remedies (such as shareholder buyouts) under judicial dissolution or intervention statutes.

4. The Value of Shares Is Not Readily Determined by a Market Price

Holders of stock in publicly held corporations can easily determine the current market value of their shares. Without an active trading market, valuing shares in a closely held corporation is much more difficult and prone to dispute. Widely accepted valuation techniques may produce very different results. Disputes over valuation can result in costly battles among valuation experts and can pose difficult problems for directors. Addressing valuation issues is an important element in preparing buy–sell agreements and is discussed in chapter 6.

5. Financial and Other Information Is Generally Not Publicly Available

Publicly held corporations are subject to the audit requirements, periodic reporting obligations, proxy rules, and other ongoing public disclosure requirements of the Securities and Exchange Commission (SEC).

In contrast, closely held corporations are not subject to SEC audit, reporting, or proxy rules, and have no public disclosure requirements imposed by market forces. Inspection rights and reporting obligations imposed on closely held entities by state corporation statutes tend to be minimal. Without legal disclosure obligations and a disciplining market, directors and shareholders of a closely held corporation have a special challenge to ensure that management supplies directors and shareholders with a sufficient flow of accurate information and that adequate programs and policies are in place to monitor and supervise the preparation of that information.

6. Deadlocks May Arise

Because of the relatively small group that typically makes up the directors, officers, and shareholders of a closely held corporation, disagreements and deadlocks are possible in management and among shareholders. Deadlocks are a special concern where ownership of a corporation is evenly divided between two segments of a family or two investor groups, each with equal representation on the board of directors. State corporation statutes provide that, upon deadlock that severely interferes with the functioning of the corporation, a shareholder may petition a court for dissolution of the corporation or other relief aimed at breaking the impasse. But dissolution may not be a practicable remedy and in any event will be lengthy and costly. To avoid the potential for deadlock, some closely held corporations include an additional neutral director on the board. Others include arbitration provisions in their articles of incorporation or bylaws or in a shareholder agreement. The benefits and problems relating to these and other dispute resolution mechanisms should be explored with counsel before adoption. There is no standard mechanism for resolving deadlocks.

7. Limited Resources and Other Practical Constraints May Result in Inattention to Corporate Formalities

The majority of closely held corporations are small businesses with very limited resources to spend on lawyers and corporate formalities. An important challenge for directors is to fulfill their duty of care to the corporation and its shareholders and to preserve limited liability for corporate participants in spite of these limited resources. Shareholders and directors in many closely held corporations may fall into the habit of taking actions in an informal manner or not recording actions in corporate minutes on a current basis. Although the law might recognize the effectiveness of such informal actions for some purposes, if an action is challenged, the burden to prove that the action was legally approved will be on the party seeking to bind the corporation. Directors may also find it difficult to establish that they were adequately informed and duly deliberate in making a corporate decision if the decision and the process leading to it have not been adequately documented in the minutes.

Informality in corporate actions; failure to keep current minutes; inattention to corporate separateness of assets, books, and records; and confusion with respect to corporate payments to shareholders can have serious legal consequences to the corporation and its shareholders. See Chapter 9 on piercing the corporate veil and other liability concerns.

D. TAX ATTRIBUTES OF CLOSELY HELD CORPORATIONS

Corporate taxation under federal and state law is beyond the scope of this *Guidebook*. Management should ensure that the closely held corporation has appropriate tax advice from counsel and accounting professionals. Difficult income taxation issues relating (among other things) to compensation and other expenses paid to shareholders (or on their behalf) frequently arise in closely held corporations. In addition, important issues relating to corporate and shareholder income taxation are often closely entwined with issues relating to estate and gift taxation and estate planning by principal shareholders of closely held corporations. These issues can become quite complex and require expert advice in the planning stages.

A few basic concepts regarding federal corporate income taxation, however, are essential to understand because, in addition to the protection from liability to outsiders and the efficient organization of governance, business owners usually desire a corporate form that will minimize their taxes. Corporate income is normally subject to dual taxation: (1) the corporation pays corporate tax on its income, and (2) shareholders pay individual income tax on corporate earnings distributed to them in the form of dividends. Noncorporate forms of business organization, such as partnerships and limited liability companies (LLCs), do not have dual taxation (although they can elect to be taxed like a corporation). Instead, partners of a partnership or members of an LLC are taxed directly on their allocable shares of partnership or LLC income, without regard to whether any earnings are actually distributed to them by the partnership or LLC. Whether dual taxation or this flow-through taxation is more advantageous for a business and its owners depends upon a balancing of many factors, such as prevailing corporate, individual, and capital gains tax rates; projected income or losses; as well as the ability to "zero-out" income at the entity level by making deductible expense payments to owners instead of nondeductible dividend distributions. Consideration of these factors as well as a variety of nontax factors is crucial in deciding whether a business should be organized in corporate or noncorporate form.

Some closely held corporations are eligible to become subject to a modified version of flow-through taxation by making an S election under Subchapter S of the federal Internal Revenue Code. Shareholders of S corporations are taxed directly on their proportionate share of corporate income and may deduct directly their proportionate share of corporate losses. S corporations do not pay income tax at the entity level. However, S corporation taxation differs in other ways from flow-through taxation of noncorporate forms and is not appropriate for many types of businesses. In order to qualify for an S election, a corporation must file an appropriate election with the Internal Revenue Service and must meet certain criteria, including having no more than a fixed number of defined "shareholders" (currently 100), no more than one class of stock, and no stock ownership by certain categories of shareholders. In all respects relating to state corporation law and to the powers and duties of directors, officers, and shareholders, S corporations are no different than corporations that have not elected this special tax treatment (often referred to as C corporations).

Although in many cases state income tax treatment of closely held corporations will parallel federal tax treatment, there can be significant differences. Management should consult with the company's accountant and legal counsel to determine applicable state income tax law.

In addition to federal and state income tax, a corporation may be required to pay annual franchise tax for the privilege of being a corporation under the laws of its state of incorporation. Some states have no franchise tax. Others require annual franchise tax payments that may be quite substantial depending upon the amount of corporate assets, income, authorized shares, and other factors used in the formula for calculating the tax in a particular state. Although most closely held corporations can effectively limit their franchise tax through proper planning, consideration of state franchise tax may still be a factor in choosing a state of incorporation.

CHAPTER 2 The Structure of Corporate Action

The basic rules of corporate governance are generally laid out in the applicable state corporation statute. Some of those rules are absolute and invariable, but many are default rules that can be varied in the articles of incorporation or bylaws or by shareholder agreement. To that end, many closely held corporations modify the default rules to fit the needs of their participants, address the lack of liquidity in the corporation's stock, and protect their multiple areas of involvement in the business (whether as director, officer, or shareholder).

A. ARTICLES OF INCORPORATION AND BYLAWS

A corporation is formed upon the filing of the articles of incorporation and their acceptance by the relevant state officials, typically the Secretary of State, Corporations Division. The articles of incorporation are sometimes called the certificate of incorporation, depending on the state, or colloquially, the "charter." The articles of incorporation establish the corporation and spell out the basic provisions required by the relevant state corporation statute, such as the name of the corporation, its agent and address for service of process, and the number of authorized shares. The articles may also contain other information regarding the conduct of the affairs of the corporation so long as such provisions are not contrary to state law.

Most governance rules in the state corporation statutes are default rules that may be changed by the participants. The articles of incorporation historically were often the only place that alterations could be made.

They still retain that function today, but most states now broadly use the bylaws or shareholder agreements as alternative sources of governance provisions (discussed in more detail in chapters 5 and 6).

Most corporations have bylaws that set out governing details of the corporation, such as the powers of the directors and officers, procedures for electing directors and filling director vacancies, and procedures for meetings of the board and the shareholders. The bylaws are typically longer than the articles of incorporation and are generally not required to be filed with the state.

In other cases, details regarding the corporation's governance may be contained in a shareholder agreement. Participants who are forming their corporation in one of the states that has not embraced a broad authorization for shareholder agreements, however, should pay particular attention to how the articles of incorporation permit alternative governance rules (or consider incorporating in another state that is more flexible in how participants can specify their alternative rules by agreement).

Together, the articles of incorporation and bylaws are sometimes referred to as the "organic documents" or "constitutive documents" of the corporation. The constitutive documents may be amended during the life of the corporation following provisions in the corporation statute of the state of incorporation.

B. DIRECTORS, OFFICERS, AND SHAREHOLDERS

1. Directors

Traditional corporate governance vests the authority to manage the corporation in the board of directors. The Model Act § 8.01(b) expresses this authority as follows: "[A]ll corporate powers shall be exercised by or under the authority of the board of directors, and the business and affairs of the corporation shall be managed by or under the direction, and subject to the oversight, of the board of directors."

Typically, state corporation statutes explicitly require that the board approve certain corporate actions, such as issuance of stock and the grant of options or rights to purchase stock. In addition to that authority, the board's oversight responsibility includes considering and acting upon other significant corporate actions, such as major debt financing, important contracts, contracts with officers, and officer compensation. The board's oversight responsibility also entails:

- reviewing and monitoring fundamental operating, financial, and other corporate plans, strategies, and objectives;
- developing, approving, and implementing succession plans for management;

- evaluating the performance of the corporation and its management and taking action—such as setting executive compensation; changing corporate plans, strategies, and objectives; or changing management—when appropriate;
- adopting policies of corporate conduct and monitoring compliance with those policies and with applicable laws and regulations as well as the adequacy of accounting, financial, and other internal controls; and
- reviewing and evaluating the process of providing appropriate financial and operational information to decision-makers (including directors) and shareholders.

2. Officers

The officers carry out the day-to-day management of the corporation. They are appointed by the board of directors and have the authority and responsibilities delegated to them by the board either in the bylaws or by specific board resolutions. Officers may also have implied authority by virtue of their titles, at least with respect to ordinary business transactions. The CEO has substantial implied authority to enter into contracts and take actions on behalf of the corporation in the ordinary course of business. Other officers may have significant implied authority in their particular areas of responsibility.

Frequently, questions arise regarding the actual authority of an officer to sign a particular contract or take a particular action on behalf of the corporation. In such cases, legal counsel may recommend that the board formally approve the contract or action and give specific authorization to the officer to avoid any uncertainty. Sometimes the other party in a major transaction or financing will require specific board approval in order to eliminate any uncertainty.

3. Shareholders

In contrast to the broad grant of authority vested in the board of directors and officers, the shareholders may engage in relatively narrow, albeit fundamental, activities. Shareholders may sell their shares, provided they can find a willing buyer, abide by applicable securities laws and are not otherwise restricted by contract from doing so. Shareholders also have the right to vote to elect and, depending on the corporation's bylaws, nominate the directors. Shareholders may also amend the bylaws and, again depending on the corporation's bylaws, put proposals forward for consideration of other shareholders. Shareholders may request inspection of the corporation's books and records and institute direct claims against the corporation or derivative litigation to enforce directors' and officers' duties.

Shareholder information rights and requests are discussed in chapter 10. Shareholder rights with respect to direct and derivative litigation are discussed further in chapter 4.

Certain other actions require both the board of directors and the shareholders to act. For example, amending the articles of incorporation and approving mergers and other fundamental transactions (statutory share exchanges, major sales of corporate assets, and dissolution) require approval of both constituents, although shareholders cannot initiate any such action. Rather, the board of directors must authorize the proposed action and bring it before the shareholders for approval.

The traditional roles of directors, officers, and shareholders may, and frequently do, vary in closely held corporations. The Model Act and most state corporation statutes allow shareholders to contract for a customized governance structure pursuant to an enumerated list of issues which shareholder agreements may address, such as eliminating the board of directors, establishing who shall be directors or officers of the corporation, and varying the voting power by or between the shareholders and directors. Chapters 5 and 6 discuss in detail modification of traditional roles and structures by contract.

C. BOARD STRUCTURE, MEMBERSHIP, AND OPERATIONS

1. Board Size and Composition

The size and composition of the board depend upon the nature of the corporation. In determining optimal size and composition of a particular corporation, consideration should be given to:

- effective performance of the board's oversight and decision-making responsibilities;
- the need for outside or unaffiliated directors to provide objectivity and independence;
- the need for a tie-breaking vote in the event of a management or board deadlock; and
- the need to represent the interests of different family factions, investor groups, or other constituencies.

Other factors that might influence board size and composition are the need of the corporation to maintain a community presence, to maintain relationships with customers or other constituencies, and to respond to other factors that may be special to the corporation or its industry. In accommodating these needs, board size should not be expanded to the point that size interferes with effective functioning.

The Model Act and most state corporation statutes permit as few as one director to make up the board and impose no qualification requirements (such as share ownership or state residency) on who may be a director. The Model Act and most state corporation statutes also permit a director to hold any and all officer positions in a corporation. In a one-person corporation (a so-called incorporated proprietorship), the sole shareholder will typically serve as the sole director and have all officer titles as well. This may be a practical necessity where permissible.

As any closely held corporation matures, it is often desirable to expand the board's composition to include individuals with varying and diverse backgrounds, abilities, experience, expertise, and access to resources that will benefit the corporation.

Many closely held corporations have recognized the benefit of having one or more outside directors. These outside directors, who are not involved in the management of the corporation, can provide independent advice, perspective, and monitoring over the affairs of the corporation and the performance of its management. Individuals who are neither officers nor employees can also bring special expertise (e.g., legal, accounting, or technical); represent important investors, customers, suppliers, distributors, or other business partners of the corporation (or otherwise help cement an important relationship); or offer some other perceived advantage to the corporation. Independent directors who are not affiliated with particular investors or business partners of the corporation can be especially useful to boards of closely held corporations as objective observers of management and business operations. The role of the independent director may be important and challenging in the context of a closely held corporation dominated by a controlling shareholder or group of related shareholders (see discussion in chapter 4).

In some types of closely held corporations, board composition reflects a negotiated balance of power among investors. The board of directors of a corporate joint venture, for example, may be made up of representatives of each of the joint venturers. The board of some family corporations may reflect negotiated numbers of representatives from each branch of the family. In corporations financed by venture capital and private equity investors or other outside investors, the terms of the financing typically include a number of board seats for representatives of the investors and a limitation on the total number of board seats. Desired board composition in these balance-of-power situations is ensured through voting agreements or use of different classes of stock, each having the right to elect a specified number of directors. In these situations, one or more independent directors—unaffiliated with any particular faction or constituency—may often provide helpful mediation of differences.

2. Board Committees

Although the board must always retain ultimate oversight responsibility, state corporation statutes and bylaws of corporations generally provide authority for the board to create committees of directors and delegate to such committees (with some limitations) the authority of the full board. Many corporations may have standing committees to oversee such matters as the audit of the corporation's financial statements, officer compensation, and corporate governance. Standing committees are less common in closely held corporations and are not legally mandated.

In addition to standing committees, boards may also create temporary committees for specific purposes. For example, a committee of disinterested directors may be formed to pass on a conflict of interest transaction between the corporation and a director, officer, or controlling shareholder. Committees of disinterested directors may also be formed to pass on the advisability of bringing suit in the name of the corporation against a director or officer when a demand for such a suit has been made by a shareholder. Special committees such as these are less common in closely held corporations than in publicly held corporations but may serve useful purposes in both types of corporations.

3. Honorary Directors, Advisory Boards, Board Observers, and Monitors

Recognizing that not all individuals are willing or able to assume full responsibilities as directors, some corporations appoint valued advisors as honorary directors or make them members of an advisory board. It is relatively common for lenders, venture investors, and other financial or commercial partners with substantial interests in a corporation to negotiate to have a representative sit in on the corporation's board meetings as an observer or monitor rather than serve as an actual member of the board.

Honorary directors, members of advisory boards, observers, and monitors are not actual directors and are not entitled to vote on matters considered by the board. Their rights and duties relating to obtaining board information, attending board meetings, and participating in board deliberations depend completely upon what the corporation has agreed to permit or require by contract. The following reflects general practices and terminology:

- honorary directors are typically asked to attend meetings, given board information in connection with meetings and encouraged to contribute to the deliberative process;

- members of advisory boards usually do not attend board meetings, receive related information, or participate in deliberations, and instead, such boards have their own meetings and formulate advice to be given to the board of directors on areas of designated interest or concern; and
- observers or monitors generally have the right to receive board information in connection with meetings and attend without participating in deliberations or in executive sessions.

Clear demarcations must be made between the roles of actual directors and honorary or advisory directors or observers or monitors. Special care is needed to assure that an honorary or advisory director, or even an observer or monitor, does not act as a director and unintentionally assumes director responsibilities and liabilities. In addition, if a matter subject to attorney–client privilege arises, the privilege may be lost if the meeting includes nondirectors in attendance. Because honorary or advisory directors and observers and monitors may not be bound by the same duty of confidentiality as actual directors with respect to information learned in connection with meetings or otherwise, the corporation should also ensure that appropriate confidentiality agreements are in place.

4. Considerations for Joining a Board

An individual considering an invitation to join the board of a closely held corporation as an outside director (i.e., someone who is not involved in the management of the corporation) will want to study the corporation, the board, and the share ownership, and accept a directorship only if confident of the competence and integrity of both the management and the directors of the corporation, as well as their own ability, to monitor and add value to the enterprise. An individual asked to be a director may be well advised to consider the following steps:

- meet the CEO and other top executives as well as major shareholders to review board organization and procedures, discuss the principal issues facing the corporation, and determine the attitude of management and controlling shareholders toward board activity;
- confer with any other outside directors currently or previously serving on the board;
- review the corporation's financial statements for at least the last two years;
- review corporate minutes for recent years to become familiar with the corporation's business, important issues addressed by the board, as well as the corporation's attention to corporate record-keeping and other necessary formalities;

- become familiar with the roles of the corporation's accountants and legal counsel;
- review examples of information regularly provided to directors;
- if serving at the request of an employer, become familiar with the employer's indemnification policies relating to service on boards at the request of the employer;
- become familiar with the corporation's provisions regarding limitations on director liability to the corporation and its shareholders, director indemnification articles of incorporation and/or bylaw provisions, director and officer liability insurance coverage, if any, director indemnification contracts, if any, and pending litigation that (1) is material to the corporation, (2) involves the activities of the board of directors, or (3) involves as a party an entity with which the individual is affiliated;
- become familiar with the corporation's conflict of interest policies and consider whether the individual has any present or potential conflicts with the corporation (an outside director serving as a representative of an investor, for instance, may repeatedly face difficult conflict of interest problems); and
- become familiar with the corporation's confidentiality and corporate opportunities policies.

D. BOARD ACTION

The board of directors takes action on behalf of the corporation by approving resolutions or otherwise indicating consensus with respect to matters presented to or undertaken by the board. Resolutions may be approved, or consensus recorded, at a meeting of the board or by unanimous written action in lieu of a meeting. The Model Act and other state corporation statutes require that minutes be kept reflecting in writing the actions taken by the board. Minutes of all meetings and all written actions are compiled in the minute book. See chapter 10 for a description of required corporate record-keeping.

1. Board Action at Meetings

The number of meetings a board finds necessary or useful varies with the circumstances, but meetings should be held as often as is needed to carry out the directors' oversight responsibility. Some boards prefer more frequent and shorter meetings, whereas others prefer fewer but longer meetings.

Meetings are referred to as "regular" meetings if they occur on a date and at a time designated in the bylaws or by a schedule reflected in board minutes. "Special" meetings are those called without such prearrangement. Special meetings may be called by anyone authorized to do so in the articles of incorporation or bylaws but are generally called by the board chair or the CEO.

In order for the board to take action at any meeting, a quorum must be present. Unless the articles of incorporation or bylaws provide otherwise, a quorum generally consists of a majority of the number of directors specified in or fixed in accordance with the articles or bylaws. If a quorum is present, the affirmative vote of a majority of directors present is an act of the board of directors, unless the articles, bylaws, or shareholder agreement require a greater number. Under the corporation laws of almost every state, a director may not "give a proxy" to another person or, in other words, have another director or designee vote for the director (in part because directors have duties and responsibilities that cannot be delegated—see chapter 3 for a discussion of these duties).

Generally, directors may participate in any meeting by conference telephone or any other means of electronic communication by which all participating directors are able simultaneously to hear each other during the meeting. A director participating by such electronic means is deemed to be present at the meeting for all purposes, including calculation of a quorum.

There are no required rules of procedure dictated by statute for board meetings, and it is generally inadvisable to adopt complex rules of procedure, such as Robert's Rules of Order, for board meetings. So long as fairness is observed, each board may generally conduct its business as it wishes. For boards with more than a few members, it is generally advisable to designate one of the directors as the chair to preside at meetings and to determine the pace and order of proceedings.

2. Establishing the Agenda for Board Action

The agenda setting forth matters to be discussed and acted on by the board is typically determined by the board chair or CEO. Furthermore, the board should satisfy itself that there is an overall annual agenda of matters that require recurring and focused attention.

Typically, a board will consider the following sorts of matters annually:

- nomination of directors and election of officers;
- annual financial results and selection of auditors, if necessary or desired;
- agenda for annual shareholder meetings;
- dividend policy;
- capital expenditure budget;

- management performance review and compensation of officers;
- status of financing arrangements;
- adequacy of insurance;
- corporate systems and controls and enterprise risks;
- annual tax and corporate filings; and
- designation of signing authority pertaining to financial and other matters.

Items that may be considered at quarterly or other periodic meetings include:

- progress on operational and financial plans;
- quarterly financial results;
- budgeting, financing arrangements, and funding of operations;
- transactions between the corporation and its directors, officers, or shareholders;
- litigation involving the corporation;
- proposals to amend articles of incorporation or bylaws;
- establishing fair market value of the corporation's stock for purposes of option grants or buy–sell agreements;
- corporate policies and practices related to employee safety and health, environmental protection, and product safety;
- compliance with applicable laws and regulations affecting the business;
- employee issues, such as equal opportunity and nondiscrimination policies, retirement and pension issues, and privacy concerns (including corporate policies and procedures relating to maintenance and safeguarding of computer and corporate records and monitoring employee communications); and
- long- and short-range planning.

Management may bring specific operational or personnel matters to the board's attention at any meeting or at another appropriate time in order to keep the board apprised of potential issues or to gain the board's advice and perspective. And, of course, at every meeting, the board will want to approve the minutes of its previous meeting.

3. Quality of Information for Board Decision-Making and Oversight

The quality of information made available to directors will significantly affect their ability to perform their roles effectively. Although directors who are involved with the management of the corporation on a regular basis may already have the necessary information, nonmanagement directors must make sure that they are adequately informed. Information submitted to the directors should be relevant, timely, well-organized, supported by any background or historical data necessary to place the information in context, and designed to inform directors of all material aspects of the corporation's business, performance, and prospects.

4. Board Action by Written Consent without a Meeting

The board may act by written consent in lieu of holding a meeting. Under the Model Act and most state corporation statutes, action by written consent must be unanimous. Generally, directors may all sign the same written consent, or they may each sign a counterpart copy of the same consent. Most state corporation statutes allow for electronic execution of consents.

E. SHAREHOLDER ACTION

Shareholders have the power to elect the board of directors and approve certain significant corporate actions specified by statute (e.g., approval of mergers and sale of substantially all assets). From time to time, the board of directors may additionally seek shareholder ratification of certain actions taken by the board. Shareholders take action by voting their shares to approve resolutions either by written consent or at meetings (annual or special).

1. Voting

Unless otherwise provided in the relevant state corporation statute or in the articles of incorporation, (1) each share of stock is entitled to one vote on each matter voted on by shareholders, and (2) all shares vote together as one voting group on each such matter. If a corporation has more than one class of stock (e.g., Class A and Class B common stock or common stock and preferred stock), the articles of incorporation must spell out when and how each share votes and whether the classes vote together or separately on particular matters.

The Model Act and state corporation statutes generally offer great flexibility with respect to the voting rights that may be specified for various classes of shares in the articles of incorporation. For example, the articles may provide that a particular class of stock has 100 votes per share or no vote at all, or no vote except with respect to certain designated matters. The articles may also provide that a particular class of stock votes along with all other classes with respect to certain matters but votes by itself with respect to others. State corporation statutes generally provide, however, that, regardless of what the articles of incorporation say, individual classes of stock vote by themselves on certain amendments to the articles of incorporation that would adversely affect the rights of the class. See chapter 5 for further discussion of multiclass stock.

2. Shareholder Action at Meetings

The Model Act and most corporation statutes require that a corporation hold an annual meeting of shareholders each year to elect directors and transact such other business as may be presented. Special meetings may be held to take actions at other times.

a. Calling the Meeting

Under the Model Act, the annual meeting will be held at a time and place, if any, stated in or fixed in accordance with the bylaws. Special meetings of shareholders may be called by the board of directors or by shareholders holding at least ten percent of the outstanding votes entitled to be cast (which may be decreased or increased in the articles of incorporation to a percentage not exceeding twenty-five percent of all votes entitled to be cast). Other state corporation statutes have varying requirements regarding the ownership requirement. In addition, the articles of incorporation or bylaws may designate anyone else as being eligible to call a special meeting of shareholders. In closely held corporations, modifying the default provisions on the authority to call shareholder meetings may be a significant matter to be addressed. See chapter 5 for a discussion of the agreements and arrangements that can be used to modify corporate default provisions.

b. Notice

Notice must be given to shareholders in advance of each annual and special meeting unless such notice is waived in writing. Under the Model Act, notice must be given no less than ten nor more than sixty days before the meeting date. Notice must be in writing and delivered by mail, in person or by electronic means, such as email. Notice is given at the time it is mailed with proper postage or when an email is transmitted (if the shareholder has consented to email notice). State corporation statutes vary on the use of electronic communications with shareholders, including matters such as a requirement of consent to use electronic communications. Notice of an annual meeting need not generally describe the purpose of the meeting, unless required by the articles of incorporation or bylaws. Notice of a special meeting must, however, describe the purpose of the meeting, and the meeting may conduct only such business as is described in the notice.

c. Voting by Proxy

Unlike a director, a shareholder may appoint a proxy to attend the meeting and vote their shares. Shares represented at a meeting by proxy are treated as being present for all purposes, including calculation of a quorum.

d. Remote Participation

The Model Act and most state corporation statutes permit remote participation in shareholder meetings. Such remote participation is subject to guidelines and procedures set forth by the board and certain statutory conditions intended to safeguard the integrity of the meeting. Typically, these would involve (1) verification that each person participating remotely as a shareholder is a shareholder, and (2) implementation of measures providing such shareholders a reasonable opportunity to participate in the meeting and vote on matters submitted to the shareholders. State corporation statutes impose varying levels of restrictions on virtual shareholder meetings that are entirely by remote communication and have no physical location.

e. Quorum and Approval

In order for shareholders to take action at any meeting, a quorum must be present. Generally, unless the articles of incorporation provide otherwise, a majority of the votes entitled to be cast on the matter constitute a quorum. For example, if a corporation has 1,000 shares outstanding and entitled to vote on a matter, each entitled to one vote per share, a quorum would be present if shareholders owning at least 501 shares were present. The Model Act and most state corporation statutes permit greater or lesser (usually not below one-third) quorum requirements in the articles of incorporation.

Under the Model Act, if a quorum exists, a matter (other than the election of directors) is approved by shareholders if the votes favoring the matter exceed the votes opposing the matter. Many state corporation statutes require the affirmative vote of a majority of the shares present at a meeting (or, in some cases, a majority of the shares outstanding) in order to approve a matter. Under such statutes, abstaining from voting on a particular matter at a meeting has the same effect as voting against the matter. Under the Model Act and the corporation statutes in states that follow it, however, an abstention is really an abstention, not the equivalent of a negative vote. For example, if the 501 shares present at the meeting described in the previous paragraph voted as follows: FOR 200, AGAINST 100, ABSTAIN 201, the matter would be approved under the Model Act, but not under a state corporation statute requiring an affirmative majority vote of the shares present (which would be 251 shares).

Note that some actions may require specific approvals. For instance, a state corporation statute may require approval of a merger by a majority of all *outstanding* shares or a higher percentage of votes (e.g., two-thirds).

f. Election of Directors

Generally, directors are elected by a plurality of the votes cast at a meeting at which a quorum is present. This means that, if a quorum is present, the directors receiving the highest number of votes up to the full number of board seats being filled are elected, even if one or more directors do not receive a vote equal to a majority of a quorum. This rule ensures continuity and should avoid hold-over directors resulting from an inability to get a majority vote for new board members.

Normally, shareholders are entitled to vote their shares with respect to each board seat being filled. If a shareholder owns 100 shares and five board seats are being filled, the shareholder is entitled to vote no more than 100 shares for each nominee for the five board seats. This means that shareholders owning a majority of outstanding shares are able to elect all the directors, that is, by voting their majority shares in favor of each nominee they desire.

Cumulative voting is an alternative method of voting that is designed to permit minority shareholders a possible opportunity to elect at least one director to the board. Under the Model Act and most state corporation statutes, cumulative voting is permitted only if the articles of incorporation explicitly say so. In a minority of states, however, cumulative voting is the default rule unless the articles of incorporation explicitly opt out of that provision. If a corporation permits cumulative voting, a shareholder may take all the votes the shareholder could cast for directors collectively (e.g., 100 shares × 5 board seats = 500 votes) and cast them all for one director. How many shares it takes to ensure the election, through cumulative voting, of one board member turns on a complex formula dependent upon the number of shares present and voting, the number of board seats open for election, and other factors. Every time the number of outstanding shares or the number of directors on the board changes, the minimum number of shares required to elect one director also changes. Depending on the circumstances, minority shareholders may not succeed in obtaining board representation through cumulative voting. If the shareholders have otherwise agreed to minority representation on the board, that result can instead be achieved with much greater precision and certainty through the use of multiple classes of stock or voting agreements. See chapter 5 for further discussion of these techniques.

g. Conduct of the Meeting

There are no formal rules of procedure required for shareholder meetings. For corporations with more than a handful of shareholders, it is highly advisable that the board chair or another person be designated to preside at the meeting and to determine the pace and order of proceedings. See the American Bar Association, *Handbook for the Conduct of Shareholders' Meetings*, for practical guidance on organizing and conducting shareholder meetings.

3. Shareholder Action by Written Consent (Without Meeting)

Shareholders may act by written consent instead of holding a meeting. Under the Model Act and most state corporation statutes, action by written consent must be unanimous. The Delaware corporation statute and an increasing number of other states, however, now permit less-than-unanimous written action by shareholders. In either case, shareholders generally may all sign the same written consent, or they may each sign a counterpart of the same consent.

F. CURING DEFECTIVE CORPORATE ACTIONS

Actions incorrectly taken by or on behalf of a corporation can create significant problems in the capital structure or governance of the corporation. Under the common law of many states, defective corporate actions are characterized as either void or voidable. A void act is one for which the corporation lacked the power or capacity to take. By contrast, an act is voidable if it was within the corporation's power or capacity but was not properly authorized or carried out in a specific case. Voidable acts may be cured through ratification by common law means, such as board or shareholder ratification; void acts may not—they are treated as invalid from the outset.

As common law provides no easy solutions for dealing with void acts, and the line between void and voidable acts has often been unclear and the subject of dispute, corporate statutes have become an important tool for curing defective corporate actions. The Model Act and many state corporation statutes authorize the ratification and validation of an overissue of stock or any corporate action purportedly taken that would have been within the power of the corporation but is void or voidable due to a failure of authorization. An overissue of stock refers to either a purported issuance of stock in excess of the authorized number of shares in the articles of incorporation or shares of any class or series that were not authorized for issuance in the articles of incorporation. Examples of other defective corporate actions that may be cured under statutory ratification procedures include the following: a failure of the incorporator to validly appoint an initial board of directors, corporate action taken in the absence of board resolutions authorizing the action, and a failure to obtain shareholder approval as required for certain actions.

The Model Act and states with statutory provisions concerning defective corporate actions set out procedures for correcting defective corporate acts. Such procedures supplement common law ratification and generally provide for a process that involves board ratification and notice to shareholders. Shareholder approval may also be necessary depending on the nature of the act being ratified and as required by the statute, articles of incorporation, bylaws, or any agreement to which the corporation is a party. Close attention to the relevant statutory requirements regarding the ratification process for defective corporate actions is advisable, particularly as detailed requirements for notice, quorum, and filings may apply. In addition, the Model Act and many state corporation statutes provide for judicial proceedings regarding the validity of corporate actions.

These corrective action statutes can be helpful when a closely held corporation with a record of informal governance is contemplating a sale or financing transaction and needs to clean up the corporation's records.

CHAPTER

3 Director, Officer, and Shareholder Duties and Rights

Under state corporation statutes, the business and affairs of the corporation are managed by or under the direction of the board of directors. The Model Act and the corporation statutes of most states impose upon directors legal duties to manage the corporation. Directors have a duty to act in the best interests of the corporation. In determining what is in the corporation's best interests, directors must have in mind the interests of all the common shareholders as a whole, rather than any one common shareholder or group of shareholders—even if they have been nominated or designated by a particular shareholder or group of shareholders, and even if they themselves are significant shareholders. As noted later in this chapter, this obligation can lead to legal entanglements for directors who have been appointed to the board to represent the interests of specific shareholders or other investors.

Directors fulfill their responsibility through two overarching functions: decision-making and oversight. The decision-making function involves considering and determining whether to approve specific matters or transactions. These can include the corporation's strategic plan, significant corporate policy, the appointment and compensation of the officers, and major corporate transactions, such as mergers and acquisitions and dispositions of material assets. The oversight function involves monitoring and evaluating the business and management, including corporate and management performance, risk management and mitigation, legal compliance, and the financial reporting and internal controls processes. Both the decision-making and oversight functions require directors to have a good understanding of the corporation's business, opportunities and risk profile, as well as a free flow of information about the business from management so that the directors are adequately informed. See the American Bar Association, *Corporate Director's Guidebook*, for a more extensive and practical guide to corporate directors in meeting their duties and responsibilities. Although there are significant differences between the structure and operation of a closely held corporation and a publicly held corporation, the director's duties, responsibilities, and rights do not differ.

A common feature of closely held corporations is the presence of a shareholder or shareholder group that controls the corporation. In such a situation, courts have generally imposed a duty of fairness on controlling shareholders in their dealings with the corporation they control and the noncontrolling shareholders.

A. BOARD DUTIES

State corporation statutes provide that the board of directors is the chief management body for the corporation. If the board has delegated day-to-day management responsibilities to corporate officers, the board should oversee their activities and make major decisions without usurping the officers' roles. Board duties generally are a mix of statutory and case law and are discussed below.

Whether the board has delegated management authority to officers or, as is the case with many closely held corporations, the officers also constitute the board, each director must exercise their responsibilities as a director in the best interests of the corporation and in accordance with legal standards for director conduct.

1. Responsibilities

a. Principal Board Functions

As discussed above, the primary functions of the board are to make major decisions for the corporation and oversee its management. Major decisions include those that state corporation statutes require directors to make (such as issuing shares and appointing officers) and those that the directors may make (such as declaring dividends). The board may also make decisions concerning a wide range of other matters that are not mentioned in the statute but are so significant as to be beyond the authority of the officers (such as approving the corporation's strategic plan). In performing its oversight role, the board must be proactive in identifying and addressing the corporation's potential opportunities, problems, and risks.

State corporation statutes typically do not list or define the board's responsibilities, but the board or the board's committees of a corporation normally are responsible for the following:

- selecting senior management especially the chief executive officer and other senior officers, setting goals for and evaluating the performance of the senior officers, determining their compensation, and planning for senior management's and the directors' succession, both in the long term and in the short term in case of unexpected circumstances;
- reviewing with management and approving the corporation's strategic plan and annual budget (and any major changes to or deviations from either);
- monitoring the corporation's financial and operating performance and management's attention to the corporation's financial position, liquidity, and capital needs;
- understanding the primary risks to the corporation's business and overseeing the management of those risks;
- understanding the corporation's financial statements and actively evaluating the integrity and adequacy of its internal financial controls; and
- overseeing the corporation's compliance with legal and ethical obligations.

b. Director Effectiveness

To be effective and fulfill their responsibilities of decision-making and oversight, directors must understand certain basic features of the corporation's business.

Directors must also satisfy themselves that effective systems exist for management to timely and thoroughly report information to the board regarding all these areas, and for the board and management to monitor and mitigate risk and assure compliance with law and company policy.

Importantly, directors must have in mind that they are responsible for making informed decisions in the corporation's best interests, even if they have been nominated or designated by a particular shareholder or group of shareholders, and even if they themselves are significant shareholders.

2. Legal Obligations

State corporation law, both statutes and common law, imposes legal standards of conduct that directors must meet in performing their roles. The basic standard, as set forth in the Model Act, requires a director to act in good faith and in a manner the director reasonably believes to be in the best interests of the corporation. This standard generally encompasses two distinct legal duties: the duty of care and the duty of loyalty. These duties are often referred to in court decisions as "fiduciary duties." The Model Act and many state corporation statutes set forth a statutory standard of conduct for directors, but it is generally analogous to the duties of care and loyalty articulated by courts.

a. *Duty of Care*

The duty of care requires a director to act with the level of care that a person in a like position would reasonably believe is appropriate for a member of a governing body in similar circumstances. The duty primarily requires the director to be informed and attentive in making decisions and overseeing the business. To satisfy the duty, the director must have all material information reasonably available that is relevant to the matter being considered. The question of which information is material is itself entrusted to the director's business judgment.

(1) Taking the Time to Be Informed

Directors will ordinarily meet the duty of care by reading materials provided to them, preparing for meetings, asking questions of management, and requesting and receiving other information and expert advice they reasonably believe they need to make a decision. They must also devote the time required to prepare for and attend meetings. Generally, directors are not permitted to act by proxy under state corporation statutes.

(2) Reliance on Experts, Board Committees

The Model Act and state corporation statutes generally give directors the right to rely on the information and expertise of management and outside advisors like lawyers, accountants, and other consultants, as long as the board is reasonable in concluding the matter is within management's or the advisors' competence. Similarly, a director may rely on a board committee if the director reasonably believes the committee merits confidence. Directors may also be reasonable in relying on the judgment and skills of fellow directors who have knowledge or experience in the matter at hand.

(3) Candor

A board of directors cannot have an effective decision-making process unless there is a feeling of mutual trust among directors and a collegial atmosphere that encourages candor. Directors must disclose to the rest of the board any material information concerning matters the board is considering. When trust is lacking in the boardroom, directors may find it difficult or uncomfortable to express their concerns or share views or perspectives that would benefit the deliberative process. A director who is hindered in this way may not be properly exercising the director's duty of care to the corporation, and the entire board could be faulted for lacking an effective process.

b. The Business Judgment Rule

The business judgment rule is a standard by which judges may review a decision of the board of directors that is challenged in court by shareholders acting for themselves or on the corporation's behalf. If the business judgment rule applies in a given situation, the judge will presume that the disinterested directors acted on an informed basis, in good faith and in the honest belief that their decision was in the best interests of the corporation. Thus, the judge will not second-guess the board's decision, even if it turned out to be wrong or unwise.

The business judgment rule does not apply in every situation. Depending on the circumstances (e.g., there is a conflict of interest), a higher standard of review may apply, which could require a director to prove affirmatively the fairness of the director's conduct. In such situations, some state courts have applied standards of "enhanced scrutiny" or "entire fairness" (see Section C of this chapter). If a shareholder is successful in its claim against one or more directors for breach of their duties, the directors may be personally liable to the corporation or to the shareholder directly.

Importantly, the business judgment rule only protects directors in claims alleging a breach of the duty of care. It does not protect conduct constituting a breach of the duty of loyalty, and state corporation statutes may not permit the shareholders to exonerate the director from liability or provide indemnification for a breach of the duty of loyalty. Chapter 9 includes a discussion of limitations of director liability and indemnification provisions for directors.

c. Duty of Loyalty

The duty of loyalty has two components: directors must act "in good faith," and they must avoid conflicts of interest with the corporation.

(1) Good Faith

The requirement to act "in good faith" means directors may take action only if they have a good faith belief that the action is in the best interests of the corporation. If a director acts in bad faith, or if the director intentionally or knowingly disregards such duties or responsibilities, the director fails to act in good faith. This can happen when the director:

- intentionally or consciously acts with a purpose other than advancing the corporation's best interests, for example, by acting in the director's personal best interest;
- fails to act when the director knows there is a duty to act, or even failing to act due to the director's conscious disregard or extreme inattention to the director's duties;
- intentionally or consciously fails to respond to "red flags," or intentionally or consciously disregards internal controls or other systems designed to detect fraud, illegality, misconduct, or impropriety; or
- acts in a manner that intentionally or consciously disregards applicable law.

(2) Conflicts of Interest

Because directors owe duties to the corporation, they must not use their positions for personal gain. Directors should also take care to avoid even the appearance of conflicts of interest with the corporation.

Conflicts of interest are not, however, inherently improper or prohibited. In fact, particularly in closely held corporations, they are often unavoidable. A director may have a direct or indirect financial or other interest in a matter that the board is considering, such as an ownership interest in another entity that proposes to provide products or services to the corporation. In such a case, the director is considered "interested" in the transaction. A director may also be "interested" when a relative or associate has an interest in a transaction, and that interest could impair the director's ability to be impartial when voting to approve the transaction.

"Interested directors" should disclose their conflicts of interest to the board along with all the relevant facts. The Model Act and many state corporation statutes provide for a procedure the board may follow to validate the transaction even when a director has a conflict. Procedures vary but typically require disclosure of the conflict by the interested director and approval by a majority of the disinterested directors or majority of the disinterested shareholders. The procedure may require that the board deliberate and vote on the matter outside of the presence of the interested director. If the board follows these procedures, state corporation law may protect both the corporation and the interested director, as well as protect the validity of the transaction. State corporation law may also provide that even if the board does not follow the procedure, the transaction is valid if the interested director proves it to be "fair" to the corporation.

Unfortunately, these procedures may be of little use in a closely held corporation where there are no or not enough disinterested directors to validate a conflict of interest transaction under the statutory procedures. For example, a difficult conflict of interest situation can arise in a corporation that is backed by venture capital, private equity, or other kinds of significant investors. These investors in early-stage companies typically have the right to appoint one or more representatives on the corporation's board of directors. Such constituent directors owe duties both to the corporation and to the investing entity they represent. The presence of constituent directors may mean there are no independent directors on the board to represent the interests of other shareholders. As explained later in this chapter, if a shareholder brings a lawsuit challenging a decision of a conflicted board, the court may apply a heightened degree of scrutiny when evaluating the board's decision-making.

(3) Fairness to the Corporation

If validating the conflict of interest transaction under state statutory procedures is possible, the disinterested directors should seek to determine whether:

- the terms of the proposed transaction are at least as favorable to the corporation as they would be if the transaction was with an unrelated third party dealing at arm's length with the corporation;
- the proposed transaction is in the corporation's best interests; and
- the process by which the board approved or ratified the transaction is fair.

This is often referred to as the "total fairness" standard of review.

(4) Independent Advice

As discussed above, the board may rely on expert advice if it reasonably concludes that the advice is within the competence of the expert. The advice may be rendered to the corporation through an oral or written fairness opinion, an appraisal, a legal opinion or legal advice, or other forms of analysis or reports.

(5) Corporate Opportunity

Directors with interests outside the corporation may receive business opportunities that overlap with the corporation's business. These directors may have a duty to make these opportunities available to the corporation before they may pursue them on their own. Whether the opportunity is one that a director must offer to the corporation depends on several factors, and directors may be well advised to consult their own legal counsel before pursuing the opportunity themselves. If an interested director has reason to believe that they must defer to the corporation, generally the director must disclose the opportunity and all material facts to the board. If the disinterested directors waive the opportunity on behalf of the corporation, the interested director is free to pursue it. The Model Act and some state corporation statutes allow a corporation to modify or exclude corporate opportunity obligations by provisions in the corporation's articles of incorporation or bylaws.

(6) Inquiry

Under both the duty of care and the duty of loyalty, directors should be alert and inquire about potential problems or events that merit board attention. For example, a failure of the board to develop appropriate information systems for reporting regulatory compliance problems to the board can be so egregious that it constitutes a breach of the board's duty of loyalty. Directors should actively and affirmatively inquire about key risk areas and seek input from appropriate experts.

(7) Disclosure

Directors should not mislead or misinform shareholders. They also have an affirmative duty to provide shareholders with all relevant, material information when asking the shareholders to vote on the proposed corporate action (e.g., voting to approve a merger).

d. Confidentiality

Directors must keep confidential all material corporate information that is not available to the public. This includes information about the corporation's business strategies and plans, trade secrets, and proprietary and other competitive information. Directors should not share the corporation's confidential information even with their family members unless the board authorizes the disclosure.

Constituent directors appointed to represent specific shareholders may share corporate information with the shareholder they represent as long as doing so would not be a breach of their duties to the corporation. This will depend on the circumstances, including the type of information to be shared, whether its disclosure would harm the corporation, and whether the shareholder has an interest adverse to the corporation. A confidentiality agreement between the corporation and the shareholder may be desirable and can help protect the parties and the constituent director. Venture capital and private equity investors can sometimes have representatives on the boards of two or more portfolio companies that are direct competitors. In those situations, the investing firm can protect the confidential information of each portfolio company by walling off communications about sensitive information between the representatives who sit on competing boards.

B. BOARD INFORMATION RIGHTS

Directors are entitled to any and all corporate information and records. Their access to this information is essential to fulfilling their duties to the corporation. Directors are also entitled to inspect the corporation's facilities, receive timely notice of meetings in which they are participants, receive and comment on meeting minutes, and have access to key employees, including any in-house legal counsel, as well as outside advisors, particularly the corporation's primary outside attorney and its auditor or accounting advisor. The board may also retain its own outside legal counsel and other expert advisors who are independent from the corporation's regular advisors. Chapter 10 has a further discussion of directors' rights with respect to a corporation's books and records. Such rights can be limited or restricted when the director has a conflict of interest.

C. EXTRAORDINARY TRANSACTIONS

Transactions that result in a change of control of the corporation are often more likely to involve a director conflict of interest than ordinary board decisions. This may be especially true in a closely held corporation where one or more directors own enough stock to control the decision to sell the company or where directors will be a part of the acquiring group. Directors in such situations will be subject to a greater degree of scrutiny than they face when making ordinary business decisions. In some states, unless the board's decision is approved by a majority of the disinterested shareholders, the directors will not have the benefit of the deferential business judgment rule.

Because state corporation statutes and case law arising from court decisions on the duties of directors in such situations differ by jurisdiction, this section will discuss general legal principles that arise in sale transactions. Directors should consult with legal counsel early in the deal process about the corporation law of the company's state of incorporation and how to minimize the risk of claims from shareholders who are unhappy with the transaction.

1. Sales of Control

Directors should review any unsolicited proposal to acquire the corporation carefully and deliberately, and in most cases should consult with financial and legal advisors in vetting a proposal. Generally, however, directors do not necessarily have a duty to enter into discussions, negotiate or sell the corporation, no matter how favorable the offer is. As long as they are adequately informed and have no conflicts of interest, the business judgment rule will apply to the directors' decision to pursue or reject an offer. The board is entitled to weigh its strategic alternatives for the corporation over the short, medium, or long term, because the board's focus on a particular time frame is itself a matter that the board may decide in its business judgment.

Once the board decides to sell the corporation or substantially all of its assets, it has a duty under the corporation law of many states to seek the best value reasonably attainable for the shareholders. This duty applies only if the consideration will be paid primarily in cash such that the shareholders will not have a significant interest in the corporation after the transaction. In determining what is the best value, courts have considered not only the price but also other terms and contingencies associated with the offer such as the form of consideration, availability of financing to fund the acquisition, the likelihood that the deal can be completed, and the risk that any required regulatory approval will not be obtained. State corporation statutes and case law vary with respect to whether the board may take into account the interests of non-shareholder constituencies like employees, customers, and the community.

There are several ways a director could have a conflict of interest in a sale of control transaction. The deal terms may provide that directors will have a continuing ownership interest in the corporation after the sale; directors may receive (or may represent shareholders who receive) benefits in the transaction that are not shared by all shareholders proportionately, or directors may be part of the acquiring group. Preferred shareholders may have contract rights that cause their interests in a sale to diverge from those of the common shareholders, which creates a conflict of interest for the preferred investors' representatives on the board. For example, preferred shareholders may have a liquidation preference that provides them first payout and causes them to have little incentive to spend time and effort negotiating for a higher purchase price so that there are proceeds remaining to distribute to the common shareholders as residual claimants. When a conflict exists, the nonconflicted directors, if any, should structure and control the sales process. Sometimes the conflicted directors will recuse themselves from the process, or the board will form a committee of nonconflicted directors to oversee the process.

It could also be important that the board's (or the committee's) advisors are independent and do not have relationships with the parties to the transaction that could impair the exercise of the advisors' independent judgment. This may require that legal counsel other than the corporation's regular corporate legal counsel and independent financial advisors be engaged to represent the board or the committee, or that the nonconflicted directors take steps to manage the conflict to prevent it from affecting the process. Under Delaware case law, which may be persuasive in the courts of other states, as a general rule, if a transaction is approved by holders of a majority of the disinterested shares in a fully informed vote that has not been subject to coercive influence by the board or management, the business judgment rule will apply, and the directors will be entitled to a presumption that they acted properly.

2. Controlling Shareholder Transactions

Sometimes a controlling shareholder attempts, either alone or with a buyer group, to purchase all the corporation's shares that it does not own. Under Delaware law, these transactions are subject to a stringent standard of review referred to as the "entire fairness" standard. Courts view these transactions as involving an inherent conflict between the personal interests of the controller or the conflicted directors and those of the other shareholders. Accordingly, the board is not entitled to the normal presumptions that apply under the business judgment rule, and instead the controller and the conflicted directors must show that the price and the process by which it was determined met the "entire fairness" standard.

To avoid the difficulty of meeting this high burden and obtain business judgment rule review, a controlling shareholder may condition the deal on the approval of a committee of nonconflicted directors and the holders of a majority of the shares that are not associated with the controller in a fully informed vote. The Model Act has an alternative means of approving a conflicted transaction, allowing for either a majority of "qualified directors" or a majority of votes cast by the holders of "qualified shares" to approve the conflicting transaction. As discussed above, the difficulty for a closely held corporation is that often there are not enough disinterested directors to validate a conflict of interest transaction under the statutory procedures.

D. DUTIES OF CONTROLLING SHAREHOLDERS

A common feature of closely held corporations is the presence of shareholders or affiliated groups of shareholders that control the corporation, often referred to as "controlling shareholders." Ownership of a majority of voting rights can give absolute control. Effective working control of a corporation may, however, be held by an individual or a group of allied shareholders, even with ownership of less than a majority of voting rights, through contractual rights negotiated among shareholders or provisions in the articles of incorporation or bylaws of the corporation that require assent of a designated class or a supermajority shareholder vote to take significant corporate actions.

Courts in some jurisdictions have imposed a duty of fairness on controlling shareholders in their dealings with the controlled corporation and its noncontrolling shareholders. Some courts have referred to this duty as one of "entire fairness," encompassing both a duty of substantive fairness (i.e., fair price) and procedural fairness (i.e., fair dealing and full disclosure). Recognition of this duty of controlling shareholders varies by jurisdiction so reference to the specific law in the applicable jurisdiction is important.

Typical contexts in which this duty has been asserted include when controlling shareholders (1) enter into an important contract with the controlled corporation, (2) propose to eliminate the noncontrolling shareholders by means of a "freeze-out" merger, (3) propose to have the corporation buy back securities from the controlling shareholder and not from the noncontrolling shareholders, or (4) pursue an opportunity that may be deemed to be a corporate opportunity. In such events, a noncontrolling shareholder may challenge such transaction as inconsistent with the duty of entire fairness. In such a challenge, the controlling shareholders and the directors approving such a transaction must prove that the transaction meets the standards of substantive and procedural fairness. A court may enjoin the transaction or award damages equal to the difference in value between the challenged transaction and a fair transaction. If the corporation or controlling shareholder, however, is able to demonstrate that the challenged transaction has been approved by disinterested directors, or by a majority of noncontrolling shareholders after full disclosure of all material information, courts have held that the burden shifts to the challenging shareholders to prove the transaction was not fair or that it failed to meet other standards determined by the court.

For these reasons, boards should generally seek disinterested director approval of significant transactions where a conflict of interest may exist between the interests of noncontrolling shareholders and those of controlling shareholders. In doing so, a board should also consider whether approval by the noncontrolling shareholders would be appropriate even if shareholder approval is not required for the transaction.

Some transactions that create such conflicts include freeze-out transactions (where minority shareholders are forced out of the corporation), transactions with controlling shareholders to purchase property from or sell it to the corporation, personal use of corporate assets, controlling shareholder pursuit of opportunities that could have been relevant and valuable to the business of the corporation, and decisions as to compensation of controlling shareholders employed by the corporation. The board should seek the advice of legal counsel in structuring disinterested approval of controlling shareholders' transactions that raise potential conflicts.

E. FINANCIAL DISTRESS SITUATIONS

When a corporation is insolvent (or in some states, when it is close enough to insolvency to be in the "zone of insolvency"), the directors may owe duties to both the corporation's creditors and its shareholders. Creditors may claim that directors acted in the interest of shareholders to the detriment of creditors, and shareholders may claim that directors were too conservative in managing the corporation's solvency risk such that shareholders were deprived of value.

Directors of financially struggling corporations should be alert to circumstances that may render the corporation insolvent or in the zone of insolvency so they know the point at which creditors are owed duties by the directors. The corporation's insolvency also affords creditors with other protections under federal and state bankruptcy laws, and violations of these laws by the insolvent corporation can give rise to claims against directors for breaches of their duties. The Model Act and state corporation statutes generally make directors personally liable for dividends or other distributions paid to shareholders while the corporation was insolvent (i.e., the corporation's liabilities exceed its assets or the corporation is unable to pay its obligations in the ordinary course), so boards of struggling corporations often obtain a solvency opinion from an independent financial advisor before authorizing dividends or other distributions to its shareholders. See chapter 7 for a discussion of dividends and other distributions to shareholders.

The risks of creditor and shareholder claims in distressed corporations underscore the importance of avoiding or appropriately managing director conflicts of interest, being fully informed and making decisions in the overall best interests of the corporation.

F. OFFICER DUTIES

As a general proposition, corporate officers owe the corporation the same overall duties of care and loyalty as do directors. Moreover, because in the closely held corporation the same person may be both an officer and a director, courts often may not distinguish between these capacities when analyzing duties. The Model Act articulates a general standard of conduct for officers that is very similar to the standard for directors. In this context, the term "officer" refers to those in whom executive or senior administrative functions are entrusted and does not apply to those without judgment or discretion as to corporate matters. An officer's duty of loyalty is of general applicability but most frequently affects officers in the areas of corporate opportunity, competition with the corporation, and the use of corporate trade secrets. Officers must refrain from doing anything of a self-dealing nature that would cause loss to the corporation. Relatively, few cases involve claims against a corporate officer for a breach of their duty of care, and the business judgment rule should protect officers as well as directors against such claims. Officers should be aware that their duty of care includes the obligation to inform the board or a superior officer of any activity that comes to the officer's attention that appears to affect the corporation's best interest.

CHAPTER

4 Shareholder Remedies

Given the illiquid nature of equity investments in closely held corporations and often the presence of other relationships with the corporation, such as employment, are there remedies available to minority shareholders in the event of abuse of power or oppression by the majority shareholder(s)? This chapter reviews potential statutory and case law remedies in such circumstances, but such remedies are highly dependent on the corporation's state of incorporation.

A. STATUTES PROVIDING SHAREHOLDERS A JUDICIAL ROUTE TO LIQUIDITY FOR OPPRESSION

All state corporation statutes have provisions for the involuntary dissolution of corporations by judicial proceeding in defined circumstances. Typically, these circumstances, as they relate to shareholder suits, involve director and shareholder deadlock situations resulting in harm to the corporation, waste of corporate assets, and abuse of power by controlling directors or shareholders that is illegal, oppressive, or fraudulent as grounds for the dissolution. Many state corporation laws also provide shareholders who have been significantly oppressed by majority shareholders with a right to seek judicial relief that can produce a buyout or similar liquidity for their shares without the dissolution of the corporation. The remedy for oppression is not automatic, but there is a predictable pattern of statutory provisions and/or case law providing when relief is available. However, even in states with clear oppression remedies, the process typically involves litigation and can be lengthy and expensive for the shareholder seeking this remedy.

Although oppression remedies in state corporation statutes are usually written to be applicable to any corporation, large or small, they generally have only been used in closely held corporations. The remedies generally are not relevant to publicly held corporations because of the liquidity of publicly traded shares and the usually passive involvement of shareholders.

1. The Definition of Oppression

Most state corporation statutes do not specifically define the "oppression" that is the basis for relief under dissolution or similar statutes, leaving the definition to the courts on a case-by-case basis. The term is often paired with "illegality" or "fraud" as the statutory standards of conduct which are the basis for the judicial dissolution of the corporation or grant of an equitable remedy. Note, however, that those terms are distinct, and the conduct that results in oppression need not be illegal or fraudulent. Some recent amendments to state corporation statutes have used "unfairly prejudicial" or other similarly expansive language. The most common definition of "oppression" used by courts in these states is when the shareholder's reasonable expectations as a shareholder are being thwarted by the majority shareholders or where the majority shareholders have behaved in a manner that is "burdensome, harsh, or wrongful" toward minority shareholders. Some states have used breach of duties as possible alternative standards. These states have corporation statutes that expressly direct their courts to take into account the duty which all shareholders owe one another to act in an honest, fair, and reasonable manner in the operation of the corporation.

2. Statutory and Judicial Sources for Remedy

Overall, the oppression remedy for shareholder dissension in a closely held corporation rarely results in the dissolution of the corporation and instead results in some other remedy to the minority shareholder. Many statutes, such as the Model Act, expressly provide for buyouts of the plaintiff's shares at the election of the corporation or other shareholders as a statutory remedy for oppression instead of dissolution of the corporation. Other judicial dissolution statutes without specific buyout provisions provide that the courts may, upon finding the statutory grounds for dissolution, issue such orders as "justice and equity" may require. Decisions in many states cite the court's general equitable power to provide relief not mentioned in the statute or to permit the court to fashion a less drastic remedy than dissolution.

3. Statutory Option for Corporation or Shareholders to Purchase

About half of the states with oppression statutes follow the Model Act in providing the corporation or a shareholder with the option to purchase all of the shares owned by the petitioning shareholder at fair value. The parties typically are given a short period to agree on the value and the purchase terms, with the court authorized to determine the fair value if the parties do not agree. These "election to purchase" statutes often are specific on the day as to which the valuation is to be determined—usually the day before the lawsuit was filed—but also provide discretion for another date that the court determines to be equitable. These statutes often permit the court to authorize installment payments, specify provisions for security to assure payment, and, if necessary, allocate the purchaser's shares among shareholders if multiple shareholders have sought to make the election to purchase.

4. Valuation

"Election to purchase" statutes provide more guidance as to valuation and related questions than general statutes authorizing other equitable relief for oppression in a dissolution context by typically using the term "fair value" for the purchase price to be paid for the shares. Generally, however, neither the traditional general dissolution statutes nor the "election to purchase" statutes provide any further guidance on how to determine fair value.

Without an active trading market, valuation of shares in a closely held corporation is much more difficult than valuation of shares of a publicly held corporation. Widely accepted valuation techniques may produce very different results. Disputes over valuation typically result in costly battles of valuation experts and can arise in many different contexts, posing difficult problems for directors.

One important valuation question is whether the valuation should reflect discounts for a minority position or for lack of marketability of shares in the closely held corporation. Such discounts are used in some financial settings and were common in early oppression cases. The discount issue has received extended discussion in the appraisal or dissenter's right context where states provide a right to a judicial fair valuation upon the occurrence of certain fundamental corporate changes such as mergers. Modern appraisal statutes more commonly provide that valuation should not be reduced by minority discounts or discounts for lack of marketability. Such reasoning may be extended to oppression suits where a court refuses to impose a minority discount when there is a finding of oppressive conduct by the controlling shareholders.

B. BREACH OF DUTY AS A BASIS FOR RELIEF IN DISPUTES AMONG SHAREHOLDERS

Shareholders of closely held corporations who believe that they, or the corporation, have suffered a loss or injury because of the actions or breach of duties of directors, officers, or controlling shareholders may seek judicial relief through a common law action alleging breach of duty. In substance, a proceeding in a statutory oppression case may look a lot like a breach of duty claim under common law. Key points of overlap are discussed here, first with respect to claims arising under oppression statutes and then in the context of lawsuits arising in the few states that do not have oppression statutes.

1. Breach of Duty in Resolving Claims Made under an Oppression Statute

As mentioned above, most state corporation statutes do not specifically define the "oppression" that is the basis for relief under dissolution or similar statutes, leaving the definition to the courts on a case-by-case basis based on various standards. Courts usually recognize that the statutory standards are not contradictory, but rather are different ways of expressing the factual context that will lead a court to look beyond the usual default rules of centralized control, majority rule, and the illiquidity of shareholder capital to provide relief when there has been oppression.

2. Breach of Duty in a State without an Oppression Statute

States that have not included oppression provisions in their corporation statutes often have case law that provides relief based on the breach of shareholder duties in the closely held corporation context. In a closely held corporation where one person or group makes the governance decisions, a falling out among the participants may leave the minority holder at the mercy of the majority. State courts in this setting have recognized the difficulty a minority shareholder will face in challenging dividend or employment policies or getting their capital out of the corporation. Because of the trust and confidence essential to this type of enterprise and the inherent risk of oppression to the minority, these courts have recognized an enhanced fiduciary duty of "utmost good faith and loyalty" that provides a buyout in specific circumstances. The duty applies not just to directors and officers but has also been extended to controlling shareholders. Although some courts have declined to embrace a different rule for closely held corporations as discussed in the prior part of this chapter, "fiduciary" duty-based reasoning has provided a route to relief in some of the states where there is no oppression statute.

3. Direct and Derivative Suits Alleging Breach of Duty

Breach of duty claims may be direct or derivative. Direct actions include, for example, claims made by an individual shareholder against the directors or officers who have made a decision on behalf of the corporation to terminate a minority shareholder's employment or eliminate dividends or payments that have traditionally been shared by all participants. Direct actions may be brought by shareholders for their own benefit for acts by directors, officers, or controlling shareholders to eliminate or reduce the value of the claimants' investment in the corporation, or their ability to exercise their rights as a shareholder to vote. These claims may also be brought under federal or some state securities laws where individual shareholders believe that they have suffered loss in making decisions to buy or sell shares in the closely held corporation because of reliance on false or misleading statements, or in some cases omissions, by directors, officers, or controlling shareholders speaking for the corporation.

Shareholder plaintiffs may also bring breach of duty claims as derivative actions. In these cases, the shareholder plaintiffs bring suit in the name of the corporation seeking recovery, not for themselves as individuals but for the benefit of the corporation with any recovery going to the corporation for the benefit of all shareholders. Common bases for successful derivative claims include misuse or misappropriation of corporate assets for the benefit of certain directors, officers, controlling shareholders, or their relatives, friends, or business associates, as well as decisions by directors or officers involving bad faith that result in loss or damage to the corporation or its business.

In addition to seeking damages in either a derivative or direct action, shareholder plaintiffs may ask a court for a temporary restraining order or permanent injunction to prevent or stop a breach of duty by directors, officers, or controlling shareholders that is proposed or already underway.

There are special procedural rules in state corporation statutes for these derivative lawsuits in which one shareholder seeks to act for the entire body of shareholders. For example, statutes often require the plaintiff to first make a demand on the directors, and if the directors are not incapacitated by conflict of interest or other breach of duty, to let them control the litigation as they would do in any other corporate decision. Courts have long recognized that a breach of duty suit in a closely held corporation does not fit into that fact pattern as there often are just two parties—the group with control that makes the decisions and the minority that is being excluded. In this setting, courts have recognized the distinct individual claim of the complaining shareholder and permitted the suit to be brought directly by that shareholder.

C. APPRAISAL IN FUNDAMENTAL CORPORATION CHANGES

In some disputes between majority and minority shareholders, the majority may implement a merger with an entity controlled by the majority and in which the minority is cashed out on terms set by the majority. These transactions may come within state appraisal statutes and entitle a dissenting shareholder to go to court for determination of the fair value to be paid to the dissenting shareholder. Appraisal statutes generally provide a route to liquidity that shareholders ordinarily would not be able to demand of the corporation absent the fundamental transaction.

In addition, common law may protect shareholders who are squeezed out in such a cash-out transaction through a claim that the majority shareholder breached its duty of loyalty. In many states, shareholders may be able to choose between the statutory appraisal remedy and the common law breach of loyalty remedy (although double recovery will not be permitted). Law developed in appraisal contexts, such as valuation principles and bans on discounts for minority status or lack of marketability, has been applied in certain cases where valuation is determined in an oppression context.

The events that give rise to, and the process for dissenting and exercising, appraisal rights vary from state to state, and shareholders must follow the prescribed procedures carefully. Appraisal statutes generally require the corporation to advise shareholders of their appraisal rights in connection with the corporate actions that give rise to them. Appraisal procedures can be complex, and any shareholder who does not strictly adhere to the applicable procedures risks being excluded from the process. These procedures are not, however, available to a shareholder who simply has disagreements, even fundamental ones, with the controlling shareholders, or who loses employment or a position in management, unless an event is occurring that specifically results in appraisal rights under the applicable state corporation statute.

D. ALTERNATIVE DISPUTE RESOLUTION PROCESSES

Because litigation in a state or federal court can be expensive and may take months or years to resolve, shareholders in closely held corporations may agree to provide for other forms of resolution of claims among them or against the corporation. It is not uncommon for mandatory alternative dispute resolution provisions to be included in shareholder agreements. There are two primary types of alternative dispute resolution commonly provided for mediation and arbitration. It is also not uncommon to mandate the combination of mediation followed by arbitration, if mediation fails.

In a mediation process, a neutral person (the mediator) designated by agreement of the parties meets with, and often receives written submissions from, each party setting forth their positions and continues to meet with the parties separately, and in some cases together, in an effort to reach a resolution of the dispute. A mediation agreement generally requires all parties to the agreement to cooperate with and respond to the mediator and set a time limit for completion of the process. Although mediators may, and often do, recommend a resolution, the parties are generally not bound to accept it.

Arbitration is different in that the result is binding on all parties to the arbitration agreement. Thus, it may follow a mediation process that did not result in resolution.

Arbitration is conducted by one or more arbitrators, who may be designated in the agreement or designated by an independent arbitration organization specified in the agreement. There are a number of such organizations, including the American Arbitration Association, JAMS (formerly known as Judicial Arbitration and Mediation Services, Inc.), and the International Institute for Conflict Prevention and Resolution. It is important that the arbitration agreement is clear as to the process for selecting the arbitrator(s) and the rules and procedures to be followed in the arbitration. Each of the organizations mentioned has model provisions that can be used.

Arbitrators commonly receive documentary evidence from the parties and may hear nonparty witnesses and, in limited cases under some arbitral regimes, require production of relevant documents. Arbitrators also receive written submissions and normally hold hearings for oral arguments in which they may ask questions of the parties and their legal counsel. Unlike state or federal courts, arbitrators have not traditionally had the authority to issue temporary restraining orders or injunctions to prevent or stop threatened or ongoing actions or omissions. However, that limitation is now less prevalent, and the agreed arbitral regime may provide for injunctive relief. Under those circumstances, if a party refuses to comply with the order, judicial enforcement may be needed. Once an arbitration process is completed and the arbitrator(s) have issued an award (sometimes with a supporting opinion), under federal and most state laws, the award is binding on the parties and enforceable by a court.

The advantages of mediation and arbitration proceedings are that they are not subject to the delays of court calendars and extensive pretrial discovery, including depositions and document production, and they can be conducted privately with no public filings or access to the proceedings. Thus, they are often less costly and more rapidly resolved than judicial proceedings. Alternative dispute resolution processes can, however, be unsatisfactory remedies for noncontrolling shareholders in situations where controlling shareholders fail to cooperate, or cause the corporation to not cooperate, during the process or refuse to accept the finality of the arbitral award. Disputes among the parties, which result in delays, may also arise when the initial agreement for alternative dispute resolution is not clearly set out and key issues, such as the process for selecting mediators or arbitrators or the rules and procedures of the arbitral regime, are unclear or left to agreement of the parties when the dispute arises. In such cases, court intervention may be necessary to move the process forward, which will result in delay and possible loss of confidentiality.

CHAPTER

5 Modifying Traditional Board and Shareholder Roles and Default Corporate Structures

A. CENTRAL ROLE OF CONTRACTING

Those who manage or invest in a closely held corporation will likely be aware of the two main characteristics of a closely held corporation. First, is the inherent illiquidity of an investment in such an entity, with no ready market for the corporation's shares. As a result, minority investors are likely to find themselves "locked-in" when an intracorporate dispute arises. Second, the individuals involved in a closely held corporation often make a substantial personal commitment to the venture, which may be the primary source of personal income as well as savings for retirement. The statutory rules of corporate governance, discussed in chapters 2 and 3, put the power to manage the corporation in the hands of directors who are elected by the shareholders. This puts key decisions like the minority shareholder's employment, compensation, and exit in the hands of the majority if disagreements later occur.

Given these characteristics, planners and participants in the closely held corporation are likely to want to take advantage of the statutorily provided flexibility to modify the default rules for corporations to better fit their particular needs. Examples include using the articles of incorporation or bylaws or negotiated shareholder agreements to alter the default governance rules so that, for example, all participants are assured a seat on the board of directors or have a veto, either as a director or shareholder, to prevent certain corporate actions that may adversely impact minority shareholders. Shareholders may also wish to provide for future liquidity of their investment, as well as an exit from the business when they retire or become disabled.

The Model Act and many state corporation statutes afford flexibility to participants to modify and tailor the traditional rules of corporate governance and the roles of directors, officers, and shareholders to fit expectations and practical needs, particularly for closely held corporations whose management and share ownership are often not distinct from one another. The Model Act and most state corporation statutes provide this flexibly to be reflected in provisions in the articles of incorporation, the bylaws, and shareholder agreements.

Although many state corporation statutes may follow the Model Act approach or provide similar flexibility to modify the traditional rules of corporate governance, it is important to confirm that any desired modifications are allowed by the corporation statute of the state of incorporation. For instance, Model Act § 7.32 (discussed in more detail in this chapter) allows for private unanimous agreements among the shareholders to accomplish specific matters that are inconsistent with one or more other provisions of the Model Act, provided that the shareholder agreement otherwise complies with certain requirements of the statute (e.g., the terms of the agreement are set forth in the articles of incorporation or bylaws and approved by all shareholders at the time of the agreement or in a separate agreement signed by all shareholders and made known to the corporation). Some states, however, may not provide this level of flexibility.

B. ARTICLES OF INCORPORATION AND BYLAWS

1. Directors

The Model Act and most state corporation statutes allow the articles of incorporation and bylaws to include variations that may provide helpful flexibility with respect to directors. These variations include the ability for directors to be elected by cumulative voting, by greater than a plurality vote, by classes or specific series of shares, or through staggered terms so that all directors are not elected in the same year, as well as restricting or limiting the ability to remove a director without cause or fill any director vacancy. In addition, the power of the board of directors to act without a meeting may be restricted or the quorum requirements for a meeting, or voting requirements for action at a meeting, may be increased or decreased from majority.

The articles of incorporation may also create a safe harbor for consideration of corporate opportunities or restrict the power of the board of directors to amend the bylaws. The Model Act and many state corporation statutes allow for the board to be dispensed with entirely or its functions to be restricted by provisions in the articles of incorporation.

This type of provision represents a major change to the default rules and is discussed in section C of this chapter.

2. Shareholders

The Model Act and most state corporation statutes allow the articles of incorporation and bylaws to include variations that may provide helpful flexibility with respect to shareholder actions, including the ability of shareholders to take actions without a meeting or to hold meetings virtually. In addition, special voting groups of shareholders may be authorized and quorums for, as well as the required vote to take action by, voting groups of shareholders for all or certain actions, such as mergers, share exchanges, and domestications, may be increased or reduced.

3. Shares

The Model Act and most state corporation statutes allow the articles of incorporation and bylaws to include variations that may provide helpful flexibility with respect to shares, including dividing shares into classes and classes into series with terms, including voting rights and the number of votes per share, that can be varied among holders within a class or series so long as such variations are expressly set forth in the articles of incorporation. In addition, distributions and share dividends may be restricted or redemption of shares allowed at the option of the corporation or particular shareholders. Furthermore, the transfer of shares may be restricted or shares issued without certificates.

4. Jurisdiction of Disputes

The Model Act and a number of states, including Delaware, allow the articles of incorporation and bylaws to require that any or all internal corporate claims for relief be brought exclusively in a specified court or courts in the corporation's state of incorporation. Exclusive forum provisions allow for efficient and more predictable management of disputes that limit interpretations of the applicable corporation statute to the courts of the state of incorporation.

C. SHAREHOLDER AGREEMENTS

In addition to allowing the articles of incorporation and bylaws to alter the traditional roles of directors and shareholders, the Model Act also provides flexibility for participants to adopt shareholder agreements. Although the provisions of the shareholder agreements may be placed in the articles of incorporation and bylaws, the Model Act also allows for private agreements among the shareholders to accomplish specific matters. The following discussion focuses on the use under the Model Act of such unanimous shareholder agreements, as well as voting trusts and voting agreements, to alter statutory norms. Chapter 6 examines the use of shareholder agreements to address stock ownership and restrictions on transfer of shares.

1. Unanimous Shareholder Agreements to Alter Statutory Default Rules

a. *General Provisions*

Under the Model Act, shareholders may enter into unanimous agreements with terms that deviate from the statutory default rules regarding governance of the corporation and the relationships among the directors, officers, and shareholders. These agreements are usually entered into to reflect the business and personal arrangements among the parties. Section 7.32 of the Model Act and similar state corporation statutes provide planners of closely held corporations a set of provisions to address specific fact patterns where the statutory default provisions may be inconsistent with the wishes of the parties. An agreement among the shareholders of a corporation that complies with Model Act § 7.32 is effective among the shareholders and the corporation even if the shareholder agreement is inconsistent with one or more provisions of the Model Act. These shareholder agreements are distinct from buy–sell agreements and restrictions on transfer agreements that limit the transfer of shares of stock and are discussed in chapter 6. Buy–sell and transfer agreements do not require statutory authority for validation.

Under the Model Act, such unanimous shareholder agreements may be adopted in one of two ways. The terms may be set forth in the articles of incorporation or bylaws, provided, in either instance, that the articles or bylaws are approved by all shareholders at the time of adoption. Alternatively, the agreement may be entered into by all current shareholders and then submitted to the corporation. In the latter instance, the corporation is not, strictly speaking, a party to or bound by the shareholder agreement. Regardless of the mechanism of adoption, the shareholder agreement may be amended only by all current shareholders unless the agreement provides to the contrary.

The existence of a shareholder agreement must be noted on the front or back of the share certificates or detailed in any information statement issued in lieu of certificated shares. If the shareholder agreement is entered into when the corporation has already issued share certificates, those certificates must be withdrawn and new certificates noting the existence of the shareholder agreement must be issued. The failure to accomplish this step does not negate the validity of the shareholder agreement or actions taken in compliance with its terms; however, the purchaser of shares without knowledge of the shareholder agreement is entitled to rescind the purchase transaction.

If the shareholder agreement ceases to be effective for any reason and it is set forth in either the articles of incorporation or the bylaws, the board of directors may amend, without the requirement of additional shareholder action, either the articles of incorporation or bylaws to delete references to the shareholder agreement.

A shareholder agreement that limits the discretion or powers of the board of directors relieves the directors of, and imposes upon those persons in whom the discretion or powers are vested, liability for acts or omissions imposed by law that would otherwise exist to the extent the discretionary powers of the directors are limited by the shareholder agreement. Furthermore, a shareholder agreement that eliminates the board of directors imposes on the person or persons in whom the discretion or powers of the directors are vested the same liability for acts or omissions as are imposed by law on directors. However, the existence of a shareholder agreement under §7.32 of the Model Act is not a basis for imposing personal liability upon the shareholders for the acts or debts of the corporation even if the shareholder agreement treats the corporation as if it were a partnership or results in the failure to observe corporate formalities otherwise applicable to the matters governed by the shareholder agreement.

Under the Model Act, a shareholder agreement may, by its terms, define its period of duration. Other state corporation statutes limit the time duration of a shareholder agreement to a specified number of years. Those state corporation statutes that do not mandate a time duration may uphold time limitations imposed by an earlier statute if the existing document was entered into when the time limitation was in place, consistent with the approach of the Model Act.

A shareholder agreement authorized under a statute similar to Model Act §7.32 is not legally binding on the state, on creditors, or on other third parties. For example, an agreement that dispenses with the need to make required corporate filings would be ineffective with respect to the filing requirement. Similarly, an agreement among shareholders that provides that only the president has authority to enter into contracts for the corporation would not, without more, be binding against third parties. In this case, principles of agency, including the concept of apparent authority, would continue to apply.

b. *Specific Provisions*

Model Act § 7.32 authorizes an agreement that alters a number of provisions in the statutory governance structure.

(1) Eliminating or Restricting the Board of Directors

The dominant feature of the corporation is that management is centralized in the board of directors, with the shareholders having only residual powers to vote to elect the directors or on certain organic transactions. Model Act § 7.32(a)(l) authorizes the modification of this structure by either eliminating the board of directors or restricting the discretion or powers of the board of directors. Although the Model Act authorizes this possibility, in practice, this option contains a significant number of uncertainties and is therefore seldom utilized. For example, although it is clear that the directors of a corporation owe their duties to the corporation and are protected by the business judgment rule, there exists no defined body of law explaining what, if any, are the duties of the shareholders involved in direct management of the corporation. This creates uncertainty as to what situations their actions will be subject to scrutiny rather than treating the shareholders as voting on a principal basis where they are allowed to consider self-interest.

(2) Governing Distributions

As a default rule, the Model Act provides that the declaration of dividends, both as to the timing and the amount, are determinations made by the board of directors. Model Act § 7.32(a)(2) authorizes a shareholder agreement to alter this rule by vesting the authority to declare distributions in the shareholders, authorizing distributions that are not pro rata to share ownership, authorizing mandatory dividends, and otherwise. The Model Act, however, invalidates distributions to the extent they render the corporation insolvent on its balance sheet or the corporation is unable to satisfy its debts and obligations as they arise in the ordinary course. Accordingly, even if the shareholder agreement has altered the board's authority to declare distributions and to determine their amount, other statutory provisions place limits on such alternation. As such, irrespective of who may have the authority to cause a distribution to be made, personal liability may occur to those authorizing the distribution in violation of such statutes as well as pro rata recoupment from each shareholder who knowingly received such distribution. See chapter 7 for a discussion on dividends and other distributions.

(3) Establishing Limits on Directors or Officers

Generally, the directors of the corporation are elected by voting shareholders, either as a group or by a class. In turn, the board of directors normally appoints the officers of the corporation. A shareholder agreement may alter these and related rules. For example, without providing for a separate class of stock, a shareholder agreement could provide that one or more directors is to be elected by certain shareholders, even if those separate shareholders do not of themselves constitute a separate "class." A shareholder agreement could also provide that directors appointed by a particular subset of the shareholders may not be removed without the consent of that subset. Likewise, the term of office as a director, which typically ends at the election of a successor, may be altered. A shareholder agreement may also provide that certain persons will be appointed as officers of the corporation or that a subset of the board of directors will appoint all or certain of the officers.

(4) Governing Voting Powers

Model Act § 7.32(a)(4) allows shareholders to agree on how general or specific matters are to be handled regarding shareholder voting, director voting, and the right to apply certain weighted voting rights. This allows for a significant override of the normal corporate structure of voting both at the shareholder level and at the director level, thus allowing the parties to treat the corporation (at least for voting purposes) much like a partnership or LLC. One of the most significant departures from traditional corporate process requirements is the authorization of director proxies. Normally directors are not allowed to delegate their authority to others, but Model Act § 7.32(a)(4) expressly authorizes delegation of director authority. This authority should be exercised with caution, however, as it can result in questions as to whether that delegation is subject to Model Act § 7.32(e) which places the liability for acts or omission on the person in whom the "director" discretion has been vested and whether the proxy holder is afforded any of the director protections provided under the Model Act and state corporation statutes.

When granting rights to weighted voting of directors or shareholders, care should be taken not to conflict with any provision of the applicable state corporation statute that references a majority or other proportion of the votes of the directors or shareholders in order to avoid any unintended consequences.

(5) Establishing Terms and Conditions for Transfers, Use of Property, or the Providing of Services

Minority shareholders in a corporation may be concerned that those in control of the corporation will utilize corporate assets or property for personal benefit rather than for the benefit of the corporation and all the shareholders equally. Although a disproportionate benefit flowing from the use of corporate property may be addressed by means of a derivative action (see chapter 4), that remedy is unwieldy in cost, both financial and time, in comparison to the potential claim. Model Act § 7.32(a)(5) provides an alternative construct that allows for a shareholder agreement to provide that transactions between the corporation, on one hand, and any identified shareholder, director, or officer, on the other hand, are subject to, for example, preapproval, after complete disclosure of all proposed terms, by a particular director or subset of the shareholders.

(6) Transferring Authority to Exercise the Corporate Powers or Manage the Business and Affairs of the Corporation

Model Act § 7.32(a)(6) allows for the orderly transfer of power from one shareholder to another shareholder or to a third party. These types of agreements are often used in closely held corporations to ensure that the business enterprise is protected from unforeseen consequences in the event of an untimely death of a shareholder. This provision is also useful in providing a private mechanism, rather than the courts (such as the appointment of a receiver or custodian or judicial dissolution), in the event of a deadlock among the directors or shareholders. Often, a shareholder agreement will appoint a person who the shareholders trust to act as an arbiter in an effort to break the deadlock. See discussion in chapter 4 regarding deadlock and remedies.

(7) Requiring Dissolution of the Corporation

Absent a contrary agreement, voluntary dissolution of the corporation requires the approval and recommendation of the board of directors and a consent of holders of a majority of the shares. Model Act § 7.32(a)(7) allows for a shareholder agreement to require that the corporation proceed to dissolution either upon the request of one or more of the shareholders, thereby bypassing both the requirement of board recommendation and approval of a majority of the shares. In addition, it may provide that upon a specified event, the corporation must dissolve. Provisions of this nature are often seen in connection with ventures in which there is an anticipated liquidity event. By requiring dissolution after the liquidity event, the minority shareholders know that the corporation will wind up, liquidate, and distribute its net assets to the shareholders, rather than seeing those assets held in the corporation for reinvestment.

(8) Governing the Exercise of the Corporate Powers or the Management of the Business and Affairs of the Corporation

Model Act § 7.32(a)(8) provides broad authorization for other agreements regarding the exercise of corporate powers or management of the corporation and the relationship among the shareholders, directors, and the corporation. However, although the limits of Model § 7.32(a)(8) are broad, there are provisions of the Model Act (and corresponding state corporation statutes) that may not be overridden if they reflect core principles of public policy with respect to corporate affairs. For example, a provision of a shareholder agreement that purports to eliminate all of the standards of conduct required of directors (see chapters 2 and 3) might be viewed as contrary to public policy and thus not authorized under Model Act § 7.32(a)(8). Similarly, a provision that exculpates or indemnifies directors from liability more broadly than permitted by statute might not be valid under Model Act § 7.32 because of strong public policy reasons for the statutory limitations on the right to exculpate directors from liability and to indemnify them.

2. Voting Trusts

Model Act § 7.30 authorizes one or more shareholders to enter into voting trusts. In a voting trust, the right to vote the shares (as distinct from the right to receive interim and liquidating dividends) is vested in a trustee. By placing the shares in a voting trust, during its term, and subject to the terms of the trust agreement, the trustee will determine how the shares will be voted. The statute imposes a number of affirmative requirements, including notice to the corporation as to the placement of the shares in the voting trust in order for the corporation to register the shares in the name of the trustee. The applicable state corporation statute may provide for a limited term for the voting trust, such as ten or fifteen years, or there may be no term limitation as is the case in the Model Act. A voting trust has a number of useful applications. For example, with respect to shares transferred from a senior generation to a junior generation, a voting trust may be utilized so that the senior generation will retain the voting power and in so doing avoid it being broadly held and thereby diluted. A voting trust may also be used by a group of shareholders to ensure that all of their shares will be voted as a block, including subsequent to a transfer of those shares.

3. Voting Agreements

The Model Act provides that two or more shareholders may enter into a voting agreement in which they agree to vote their shares in particular ways to effect agreed-upon changes in corporate governance. For example, three entrepreneurs may decide to incorporate and agree that each will be an equal shareholder. One of the most common expectations in such a situation would be that each of the three would serve on the board of directors so long as they remain an owner and involved in the business. In this regard, the traditional corporate structure could fail them without modification. In the event that the three had a falling out, two with majority voting power could join forces to remove the third director from the board. Using a voting agreement, the expectations of the shareholders could be captured by having the three shareholders agree that, so long as each remains a shareholder, they will vote their shares in such a manner as is necessary to keep all three on the board. Note that such agreements need not be among all shareholders and would not require the kind of validation that is required in Model Act § 7.32.

D. OTHER COMMON ARRANGEMENTS

1. Cumulative Voting

Cumulative voting for the board of directors is provided for in Model Act § 7.28. Under cumulative voting, the otherwise prevailing rule that a plurality of the shares cast elects the entire board can be modified in the articles of incorporation such that the directors will be elected on a cumulative basis. Under cumulative voting, each shareholder is entitled to multiply the number of votes they are entitled to cast by the number of directors for whom they are entitled to vote and cast the product for a single candidate or distribute the product among two or more candidates. In effect, cumulative voting allows a minority of the shareholders to aggregate their votes and thereby increase the likelihood that a particular candidate for a seat on the board will be elected. Although it is intended that cumulative voting will enhance the ability of a minority shareholder or block of minority shareholders to elect representation on the board of directors, there is no guarantee that such will be effective as there is an interplay between the number of shares held by the minority position and the number of directors to be elected. At the extreme, if the majority of the shareholders have the ability to fix the number of directors, and that number is fixed at one, then the majority will have the right to elect the entirety of the board.

Cumulative voting is constitutionally required in certain states. In addition, certain states provide that shareholders will have cumulative voting as the default rule. Thus, whether shareholders of a corporation may elect in or out of cumulative voting is a state-specific issue. See further discussion of cumulative voting in chapter 2.

2. Multiple Classes of Shares

Another mechanism that may be employed to provide particular protections to some, if not all shareholders, is through the use of multiple classes of stock. For example, consider a family-owned company in which the shares are distributed among three lines of family members. Any one of those lines may be concerned that the other two could combine and, constituting a majority, effect a corporate transaction to which they do not approve. The shares held by the restrictive groups could be denominated

Class A, Class B, and Class C. All of the shares, irrespective of class, would have the same voting rights (one vote per share) and the same right to participate in distributions. However, by having multiple classes of shares, it can be provided in the organizational documents of the corporation (typically the articles of incorporation) that any extraordinary transaction, such as a merger, sale of substantially all assets outside the ordinary course, voluntary dissolution, and amendments to the articles of incorporation, will require the approval of not less than a majority of the shares of every class. In this way, although the various persons holding the Class A shares could, among themselves based on ownership percentage, determine whether there was majority approval for a proposed course of action, that proposed course of action could be implemented if and only if a majority of the shares held by each class of shares approved doing so. There is, however, no requirement to afford every class of shares (equal voting rights or necessarily any voting rights) with respect to a proposed course of action. For example, it could be provided that the Class A shareholders are entitled to elect four members to the board of directors, the Class B shareholders are entitled to elect two directors, and the Class C shareholders are entitled to elect only one director. These disproportionate allocations of voting authority, and thereby a voice on the board of directors, could be justified based on the level of family line involvement in the day-to-day business, disproportionate contributions made by an earlier generation of the family, or whatever is appropriate for the circumstances of the particular venture.

This *Guidebook* generally does not discuss the provisions of Subchapter S of the Internal Revenue Code or other tax provisions that may have an impact on planning and operation of a closely held corporation. However, it should be noted that closely held corporations organized as S corporations have restrictions relating to multiple classes of shares because of the "single class of stock" rule of the Internal Revenue Code and therefore should be carefully examined.

3. Preemptive Rights

Shareholders have the ability to provide for preemptive rights in shareholder agreements. A preemptive right is the right to acquire, upon issuance, that number of newly issued shares such that the shareholder may preserve its existing percentage ownership interest in the corporation. However, that will require the shareholder to invest additional capital into the corporation to acquire the additional shares to maintain their existing percentage ownership. A provision for preemptive rights can generally also be included in the articles of incorporation, but this is likely less common. Attention to the applicable state corporation statute is critical to consideration of preemptive rights. In some states, preemptive rights may be the default rule, in which case, the articles of incorporation would need to affirmatively preclude such rights if that is the desired result.

4. Veto Rights

A significant shareholder or a class of shareholders in a closely held corporation often will want the right to veto certain corporate actions. This negative control over corporate actions is achieved by requiring a class vote or the prior approval of a named shareholder before a corporate action may be taken. Venture capitalists and other private equity investors generally will require a significant degree of negative control as a condition to making an investment in a corporation. Corporate actions over which a shareholder or class of shareholders may seek a veto right include any amendment to the articles of incorporation that would adversely affect the rights of the shareholder or class; issuances of new securities; any sale, disposition, or license of the corporation's business or assets; any merger, conversion, domestication, or similar transaction; any investment in another corporation; any distributions to shareholders; approval of transactions with employees or shareholders; and other key decisions that may affect the fortune or the finances of the corporation.

Although veto rights protect against a corporation taking action without a shareholder's consent, veto rights do not give a shareholder any particular power to compel a corporate action. Even the right to appoint a director to the board will not guarantee a shareholder the ability to exert influence or control over the board's decisions. Absent the ability to control the board, a shareholder can achieve a measure of affirmative control by agreeing with other shareholders in advance on certain corporate policies (e.g., dividend or capital expenditure policies). These types of agreements are frequently contained in a shareholder agreement.

CHAPTER 6

Buy–Sell Agreements and Other Restrictions on Stock Transfers

Restrictions on the free transferability of the closely held corporation's shares can be extremely important to the governance of the corporation and the attainment of shareholder goals and objectives. Careful planning and drafting of buy–sell agreements and related restrictions on transfer are often critical to maintain the business bargain among shareholders in a closely held corporation.

A. BUY–SELL AGREEMENTS

1. What Issues Are Being Resolved?

Shares of stock in general are personal property that are freely transferable. As such, a shareholder may sell the shares to another shareholder or to a third party, and the purchaser thereafter has the rights of a shareholder. At the same time, there is generally little or no market for those who want to exit a closely held corporation.

A buy–sell agreement (otherwise often referred to as a stock restriction or stock redemption agreement) may by contract limit the ability of a shareholder to sell or otherwise transfer shares, thereby affording the shareholder group the ability to control who will be a shareholder. It may also provide that upon particular events the corporation and/or the other shareholders are bound to make a market for (i.e., agree to purchase) the stock of a shareholder undergoing the defined event. It can also provide for a right to expel a shareholder from the corporation or address tax classification elections that have been made.

Generally, a buy–sell agreement is binding only on the parties that sign it. But a buy–sell agreement may be drafted to bind subsequent holders of the shares notwithstanding that they have not signed the agreement, thus restricting the property rights of future holders of the shares.

2. The Corporation as a Party to the Buy–Sell Agreement

Although it is conceivable that some or all of the shareholders may, among themselves, enter into a buy–sell agreement to which the corporation is not a party, it is far more typical that the corporation is a party to and bound by the buy–sell agreement. Absent being a party to and bound by the agreements, no obligations under any buy–sell agreement would be enforceable against the corporation.

The corporation's agreement to be bound by the buy–sell agreement should be reflected in board resolutions: (1) approving the terms of the agreement to which it will be a party, (2) directing an officer or other duly authorized representative of the corporation to on its behalf execute and deliver the agreement, and (3) providing for it to be effective upon due execution and delivery. When the buy–sell agreement is entered into at the same time as the organization of the corporation, the board resolutions approving the buy–sell agreement and authorizing the necessary actions may be incorporated in the initial resolutions of the board of directors completing the corporation's organization.

3. The Importance of Putting the Buy–Sell Agreement in Place Early

In the initial stages of the venture, participants may be reluctant to spend time and money on a buy–sell agreement. They may rationalize that disagreements will not arise or that ancillary agreements may be put in place at a later date. Legal counsel should point out that it is important to have a buy–sell agreement in place at the time of formation—when the participants typically have similar desires and expectations. It is at this point in time, when none of the expected participants have divergent views, that the buy–sell agreement should be negotiated and put in place. Having a buy–sell agreement in place reduces the risk of needing to resolve future disputes in court.

B. RESTRICTIONS ON TRANSFER

Most buy–sell agreements restrict shareholders from transferring their shares except on specific terms. A common provision is that the shares may be transferred only to (1) the corporation, (2) other incumbent shareholders, (3) the shareholder's immediate family members, (4) entities controlled by a shareholder, or (5) entities controlled by a shareholder's immediate family members. The buy–sell agreement will typically provide that the corporation will not recognize a transfer not made in compliance with the transfer restrictions and in consequence will neither issue to the purported transferee a new share certificate nor update the share transfer ledger. See the discussion in Section R on the legal and contractual limits on the corporation's ability to redeem shares subject to bankruptcy.

If the buy–sell agreement permits sales to incumbent shareholders, it may condition that right upon notice to the corporation or the corporation and all other shareholders. The agreement may condition the right to buy/sell upon a right of first refusal afforded to each other shareholder so as to preserve proportionate ownership in the corporation. Limitations on inter-shareholder transfers are justified on the basis that those transfers may alter respective voting rights among the shareholders with the risk of undesired concentration or change in control. Consider, for example, the case where the shares of a corporation were initially held equally by four sibling shareholders, and two of the shareholders sold their shares to the third shareholder, vesting that shareholder with a 75 percent voting position. The one shareholder who had not participated in those purchases/sales objected, asserting the right to participate in those purchases/sales in order to preserve that shareholder's respective voting rights. On those facts, the court held that absent a buy–sell agreement affording all shareholders the right to participate in an inter-shareholder sale, the transaction was valid. One court considering this fact pattern made the observation that the law provides ample methods for shareholders to maintain equal ownership should they so desire, including buy–sell agreements, stock transfer restrictions, and the like.

Restrictions on transfer where the status of the possible purchaser has important regulatory or tax implications are typical. For S corporations, typical limitations on transfer include that a transfer may not be made to a proposed shareholder whose status would violate the terms of its S corporation election. Similarly, in a professional services firm, it is common to prohibit all transfers; new shareholders are to acquire shares only by issuance from the corporation, or the transfer restrictions require the purchaser be a qualified licensed professional in the jurisdiction.

Also, a typical buy–sell agreement would provide that the shares in the hands of a permitted transferee remain subject to the buy–sell agreement to the effect that the permitted transferee may not affect a subsequent transfer absent compliance with the agreement's limitations.

C. RIGHT OF FIRST REFUSAL

In the most common form of transfer restriction, shareholders are prohibited from selling shares to a third party without first offering the shares to the corporation and its shareholders. Some agreements impose these same limitations upon sales among incumbent shareholders. The buy–sell agreement will typically require the shareholder to advise the corporation of the identity of the proposed transferee, the number of shares proposed to be transferred, and the financial terms of the proposed sale. The corporation usually has the first option to purchase the shares on the same terms as have been offered to the third party. The agreement should afford the corporation's board sufficient time to review the terms and to make an informed decision on whether to exercise its purchase option.

If the corporation elects not to purchase all or any of the shares or is unable because of financial, legal, or contractual limitations to make the purchase, typically the buy–sell agreement will extend the option to the non-selling shareholders or their assignees, who may among themselves purchase the shares on a pro rata basis. The corporation and the non-selling shareholders have a specified number of days within which to exercise their right of first refusal. Thereafter, if the right of first refusal is not exercised, the selling shareholder may sell the shares to the third party. Few third-party purchasers will accept the delay and uncertainty associated with buying shares that are subject to a right of first refusal. As a result, a right of first refusal is a powerful tool to control share ownership in a closely held corporation.

Most agreements will provide that, between the corporation and the other shareholders, the right of first refusal must be exercised with respect to not less than all of the shares the current shareholder would propose to sell to the third party.

Some agreements provide that in the event of a proposed third-party sale, the option of either or both of the corporation and the other shareholders may be exercised at the lesser of the proposed sale price or a price determined pursuant to the buy–sell agreement. It could, for example, set a fixed value for the shares or provide a formula for determining the price. This approach mitigates the risk of the proposed seller and buyer negotiating an inflated price as a mechanism for avoiding the exercise of the option.

D. TRANSFERS TO FAMILY MEMBERS

Some buy–sell agreements impose a right of first refusal upon transfers by sale or gift to family members. Other buy–sell agreements permit certain transfers by either sale or gift to family members. If the buy–sell agreement defines permitted transferees to include the family of the shareholder, it needs to address whether those transfers may take place during the life of the shareholder or only upon the shareholder's death. Also, the agreement should define "family." Although a spouse and children (natural or adopted) are almost certainly contemplated by that term, does it extend to stepchildren or spousal equivalents? Does it extend to nieces and nephews? Are in-laws within the scope of "family"? If the buy–sell agreement fails to define the "family" to whom transfers may be made, litigation may result. Also, as noted above, the agreement should consider proportional family branch ownership/voting rights.

E. SHAREHOLDER DEATH OR DISABILITY

Another common feature of a buy–sell agreement is the right or obligation of the corporation to redeem a shareholder's shares when the shareholder dies or becomes permanently disabled. The agreement may also provide the disabled shareholder or the estate of the deceased member a put option that requires the corporation to redeem the shares at the value set by the agreement.

With respect to a shareholder's death, the buy–sell agreement will need to indicate the valuation methodology to be employed in valuing the shares; the timing of the redemption if, as is typical, a personal representative/executor must be appointed on behalf of the decedent; and perhaps even the need to advise that personal representative/executor of the terms of the buy–sell agreement. It also should include whether the corporation has the obligation or right to redeem the shares and the terms by which that redemption is exercised (e.g., notice to the estate), and/or the right of the estate to put the shares to the corporation. Where the shareholders (other than the decedent) have either a first or second right of first refusal to acquire the shares, or where they are personally obligated to purchase the shares under a put option, notice to them of these and related issues should be provided for in the buy–sell agreement.

In the case of any rights that are exercisable as a result of disability, it is first necessary to define when disability exists. It is common practice to do so by reference to disability insurance policies maintained by the corporation on behalf of its employees and officers. Of course, incorporation by reference of those standards should be done only after substantive review of the insurance policies and a determination as to whether they are overly restrictive. Also, if the definition of disability is incorporated from a disability insurance policy, consideration should be given as to whether that contractual methodology of assessing disability, which may require medical exams and opinions of legal professionals, is necessary or appropriate. Some buy–sell agreements will adopt the definition of disability from a company-maintained insurance policy but have a distinct mechanism (typically more relaxed) for determining whether disability exists.

Other points of potential disagreement may include whether the definition of "disability" adopted by reference to a disability insurance policy refers to the policy in place at the time the buy–sell agreement is entered into or at the time of the event that is potentially characterized as giving rise to disability. Consideration should also be given to what that definition will be if, at any particular point in time, no disability policy is in place.

F. TERMINATION OF SHAREHOLDER EMPLOYMENT

A common issue for closely held corporations is what to do when an employee owning shares in the corporation leaves its employment. Many closely held corporations view former employee shareholders as potentially disruptive. The buy–sell agreement can provide a solution to this problem by giving the corporation an option to redeem the departing employee's shares. This option is especially useful when a shareholder employee leaves the corporation involuntarily or as a result of a dispute. In family-owned closely held corporations, the loss of employment and a forced sale of stock can be particularly complicated.

In drafting buy–sell agreements, not all shares (and by implication shareholders) need be treated the same. For example, assume a corporation where all of the shares are held by heirs of the founder and not all shareholders are actively involved in management. Upon issuing shares to a non-family senior employee, it may be provided that upon termination of that person's employment, the shares will be subject to redemption. At the same time, the agreement would specify that the right of the corporation to redeem the shares upon the shareholder ceasing to be an employee is applicable only to the nonfamily employee shareholders.

G. CHANGE OF CONTROL OF AN ENTITY SHAREHOLDER

Shares in a corporation may be owned by another legal entity, such as another corporation, an LLC, a partnership, or other entity. Also, shares in a corporation may be held in a trust. In those circumstances, a buy–sell agreement should address the change of control of an entity shareholder. For example, if shares are owned by an individual, the buy–sell agreement will limit the ability to transfer those shares unilaterally. If, however, shares are held by another corporation, the sale of control of that corporation will effect a change of control of shares in the subject corporation. To address this concern, a buy–sell agreement could (1) define a "transfer" or a "change of control" to include a transfer of shares or a change of control of the business entity shareholder, as applicable, and (2) specify the consequences upon that transfer or change of control, including a right of first refusal on the shares held by the entity shareholder.

Attention should be paid as well to shares held in trust. Typically, upon a dissolution of the trust and the distribution of its corpus to the residuary beneficiaries, a right of first refusal (assuming those beneficiaries are not already otherwise shareholders in the corporation) may be triggered. At the same time, the mere substitution of one trustee for another, especially in circumstances in which those trustees are institutions, will typically, although not always, not trigger any right of first refusal or similar rights under the buy–sell agreement.

H. TRANSFER UPON DIVORCE OR DISSOLUTION OF A CIVIL UNION

Most buy–sell agreements will provide that the transfer of shares pursuant to a divorce decree or dissolution of a civil union (and division of martial property) where the shareholder party to the agreement no longer holds sole title to the shares will trigger whatever right would apply either upon a proposed voluntary transfer or upon death. A court, in determining the value of the shares in a divorce proceeding, should account for the buy–sell agreement's terms. For example, if the shares are subject to redemption at book value or another pre-determined measure of value, then in the hands of the transferee spouse the value of the shares should be not more than that amount.

It is a common practice to have the shareholder's spouse or civil union partner execute an acknowledgment and consent to the buy–sell agreement. This is particularly important in community property states. Doing so addresses a potential claim that, in the context of a divorce and property division, the buy–sell agreement is either unenforceable or inapplicable to set the value of the shares.

I. TRANSFERS TO MINORS

Because minors do not have the legal capacity to contract, it is a common provision in buy–sell agreements that no transfer to a minor will be recognized. Some agreements will provide that a transfer which would otherwise be made to a minor, such as upon the death of an incumbent shareholder, must be to a trust for the minor's benefit and impose requirements upon the trustee. Those requirements often require either that the trustee be an otherwise incumbent shareholder of the corporation or that it be an institution with trust powers.

J. VALUATION OF PURCHASE PRICE

The buy–sell agreement should have a detailed and unambiguous provisions as to the valuation methodology that will be applied upon any redemption or exercise of a put or call option by a shareholder, including the date on which the shares will be valued. The agreement should specify who will perform the valuation and the nature of the report to be provided. It can be agreed that a full appraisal report is not necessary. Furthermore, it could be agreed that the valuation will not be done by an independent appraiser; in some circumstances, the corporation's board of directors or a senior member of the finance staff may be charged to make the valuation, a mechanism especially appropriate where the valuation is based upon a formula. It needs to be specified that the valuation is of the shareholder's interest in the corporation, being separate and apart from the corporation's assets and activities. The agreement should address whether the valuation (if not a formula) is of book value, fair value, fair market value, or otherwise, and then provide clarity as to what is intended by the terms employed. For example, if book value is the measure of value, how should unrealized appreciation in assets such as real property be addressed? If fair market value is the measure of value, the agreement should reference the lack of control and lack of marketability discounts as factors the appraiser may consider so that there is no question whether the discounts are components of determining fair market value under the terms of the agreement.

In many cases, there is a distinction between fair value and fair market value, and accordingly, clarity for the intended measure of value is critical. If and to the extent that the shareholder was an officer or employee of the corporation receiving compensatory payments, for purposes of clarity, the valuation should specify that those payments are not to be included in the valuation of the shareholder's shares. For corporations holding real estate, the agreement may provide that the property shall be deemed to be valued at the last property tax assessment, or that it is to be appraised by a real estate appraiser with that appraisal incorporated into the business appraisal. These approaches also may be applied for significant equipment and machinery.

If the valuation is to be a formula, the agreement should address how the formula is determined and who determines it. If the corporation maintains life insurance upon one or more members for the purpose of funding a redemption, the agreement should explicitly address whether the cash surrender value of the policy is included or excluded in the determination.

K. PAYMENT TERMS AND SECURITY

The agreement should also provide for how the price of the shares is to be paid. The agreement may provide for deferred payout, including the required period of time for such payout, in the event that the corporation is redeeming the shares and is unable to pay the redemption price in a lump sum or needs time to generate the cash to pay the obligation. Other issues might be whether the obligation will bear interest and if so at what rate, whether the obligation to pay the redemption amount will be secured and if so by what collateral, and what limitations on interim distributions will be imposed while the redemption obligation is outstanding. Essentially, everything that would need to be addressed in a well-drafted stock restriction agreement should be included in the terms for redemption.

Some agreements will provide similar purchase payment flexibility to other shareholders who are purchasers. If the acquisition is consequent to death, it is common to provide that all proceeds of life insurance policies held on the decedent shareholder will be applied at closing to the purchase and that only any outstanding balance will be payable over time.

Where the corporation is redeeming the shares over time, some agreements provide that each payment is treated as a pro rata redemption of a percentage of the shares which are then canceled; the selling shareholder then remains a shareholder as to the remaining unredeemed shares. Alternatively, the agreement may permit the corporation to issue the selling shareholder a promissory note in which case the shares have been redeemed and the seller is a creditor of the corporation (rather than potentially remaining a shareholder). The shares may then be canceled or held as collateral for the debt obligation.

It is important to make clear in the buy–sell agreement how a shareholder whose shares are being redeemed by the corporation will be treated for purposes of shareholder rights during the period of time beginning with the redemption right being triggered through the closing of the redemption. One approach is for the shareholder being redeemed to remain a shareholder up until the time that the valuation is completed and there is a closing on the redemption itself. In this scenario, pending the closing, the shareholder being redeemed will have rights as a shareholder to vote, inspect books and records, participate in dividends/distributions paid with a record date before the closing, and initiate either a derivative action or an action for judicial dissolution, which may be disruptive to the corporation. The other approach is to treat the shareholder being redeemed as a former shareholder whose shares have been redeemed but with the redemption price to be determined. In this scenario, upon redemption being triggered, the person's shareholder rights, conceived of as property, will in effect be converted into a series of contractual rights, the most important being the right to receive the redemption price when calculated and the closing is completed.

L. CO-SALE RIGHTS/TAG-ALONG RIGHTS

Some buy–sell agreements include the right of all shareholders to participate in the sale of shares by one shareholder to a third party. This right, often referred to as a "tag-along," is particularly useful to prevent a key shareholder from selling out their interest and thereby separating from the corporation, leaving the minority owners subject to the control of the new majority owner. If the key shareholder decides to sell its shares, the other shareholders will have the right to participate in the sale and sell their shares on a pro rata basis on the same terms. By way of example, assume founder owns 51 percent of the shares, with the balance of 49 percent owned by a second shareholder. Absent a co-sale right (and assuming not otherwise barred by a buy–sell agreement), founder could sell the 51 percent interest in the corporation. Meanwhile, second shareholder would continue to have only the rights of a minority shareholder. With a co-sale provision, founder could sell to buyer 51 percent of founder's shares, while second shareholder could sell to buyer 49 percent of their shares. In doing so, the minority shareholder enjoys the same liquidity opportunity as does the majority owner.

Sometimes, the co-sale right will replace a right of first refusal. The two provisions may also work in tandem with the co-sale right arising after the right of first refusal.

M. DRAG-ALONG RIGHTS

Sometimes presented as the flip side of tag-along rights, a so-called drag-along right imposes upon all shareholders the obligation to sell their shares in the event that a certain threshold of the shareholders determines to sell. Drag-along rights facilitate stock sale acquisitions. For example, in a corporation with a single 40 percent shareholder and the balance of the shares disbursed among shareholders none of whom own more than 3 percent, a drag-along right might be triggered when 46 percent of the shares (the dominant 40 percent shareholder and at least two other shareholders) want to sell.

N. RESTRICTIVE LEGEND ON SHARE CERTIFICATES

The existence of a buy–sell agreement should be noted in a legend on the share certificates. The failure to note the buy–sell agreement may result in the agreement being unenforceable against parties without knowledge of the restrictions contained in the agreement. Some corporations will make note of a buy–sell agreement limiting the transferability of shares in the publicly filed articles of incorporation. Although a third-party purchaser may not be deemed on notice of the provision as a matter of law, if a sale is completed the purchaser will be a shareholder and presumably bound thereby.

O. INSURANCE AND OTHER FUNDING SOURCES

If the corporation is redeeming shares with the proceeds of insurance on the shareholder's life, it should be specified whether the proceeds of the policy are or are not to be included as an asset of the corporation. For example, assume a corporation is valued at $3 million. The corporation in turn has three equal one-third shareholders. The corporation maintains a life insurance policy, payable to the corporation, on the life of each of its shareholders with the intention that the proceeds of the policy be applied to redeem the shareholder's shares upon death. One of the shareholders dies, and the corporation receives the $1 million death benefit. On those facts, a provision regarding inclusion or exclusion of the value of the proceeds is critical. With exclusion, the valuation of the company would remain $3 million and not be increased to $4 million simply because it is now holding an additional $1 million in cash. Accordingly, the deceased shareholder's estate would receive $1 million. If the value of the proceeds of the policy is included in the corporation's value, however, the value would be increased to $4 million and the shareholder's estate would receive $1.33 million.

P. LEGAL AND CONTRACTUAL LIMITS UPON REDEMPTION BY THE CORPORATION

A corporation's redemption of its own shares will typically be treated as a distribution to the shareholder being redeemed. Typically under state corporation statutes and particularly under the Model Act, both a balance sheet and a cash flow solvency test must be satisfied in order for a distribution to be proper. Some agreements provide that if the corporation is unable to effect the redemption under these statutory limitations, the remaining shareholders, in place of the corporation, must effect the redemption. Other agreements may provide that, when the corporation is unable to effectuate a redemption due to the legal restrictions on its ability to make a distribution, the corporation's obligation to perform is stayed until such time as the redemption may proceed. The board making the redemption decision must be able to satisfy the solvency tests at the time of the redemption decision. If the redemption of the shares is deemed to be made in installments over time and the redemption of a portion of the shares is only made when payments are made, then the board must make the determination each time. Alternatively, the legal validity decision can be made just once with a complete redemption of the shares with the price paid over a period of time pursuant to a promissory note (including consideration of the note terms in applying the asset and cash flow tests). In that situation, the redeemed shareholder thereafter is a creditor of the corporation rather than a shareholder.

Even where the statutory limits are satisfied, a corporation, in effecting a redemption, must assure itself that doing so does not violate restrictive covenants in other documents. For example, it is a common loan agreement covenant that, while the loan is outstanding, the corporation borrower may not redeem any equity.

Q. BUY–SELL AGREEMENTS AND ACTIONS FOR JUDICIAL DISSOLUTION

Under the corporation laws of certain states, a minority shareholder may move for judicial dissolution of a corporation on the grounds of "oppression," sometimes characterized as a determination that the shareholder's reasonable expectations as a shareholder are being thwarted by the majority shareholders. In some states, the existence of a buyout right may obviate the risk of a shareholder bringing an action for judicial dissolution where the shareholder has the right to withdraw from the corporation and receive a liquidating distribution. See chapter 4 for further discussion of this topic.

R. THE BUY–SELL AGREEMENT IN BANKRUPTCY

There is little concrete guidance on the treatment of a buy–sell agreement in the bankruptcy of an individual shareholder. It may well be that this absence of concrete guidance is due to the individual facts of various bankruptcies as well as the peculiarities of the particular buy–sell agreement implicated. It should be expected that provisions of the buy–sell agreement triggered by bankruptcy, such as one providing that the corporation shall have a right to redeem the shares upon a shareholder's personal bankruptcy, are subject to avoidance by the bankruptcy court.

A buy–sell agreement may provide that, in the event of a shareholder's bankruptcy, the shares will be appraised at either fair value or fair market value by an independent appraiser, and thereafter be subject to redemption. Where there is an independent appraisal of the shares at either fair value or fair market value, enforcement of the buy–sell agreement and the right to redeem shares from a bankrupt shareholder may be more likely to be enforced. In that circumstance, however, it may be important to provide that this is simply a call option exercisable by the corporation, rather than a put that may be exercised by the bankrupt shareholder and, if applicable, a trustee in bankruptcy.

In almost all circumstances, a corporation that is in bankruptcy will fail either or both of the solvency tests discussed above. Consequently, the corporation will not be able to perform on any obligation under a buy–sell agreement to affect the redemption of shares. In addition, upon entering bankruptcy, if and to the extent the corporation is in the course of redeeming shares—for example, pursuant to performance on a promissory note delivered at closing—that performance will be suspended.

S. SURVIVABILITY OF OTHER OBLIGATIONS

Many buy–sell agreements will contain a variety of other agreements that impose limitations on the shareholders not directly related to the purchase or sale of the shares. These limitations within the buy–sell agreement may be applicable for varying periods of time or indefinitely after the closing of the purchase or sale. These limitations can include (1) noncompetition covenants, (2) nonsolicitation of customers, (3) nonsolicitation of employees and other service providers, and (4) restrictions on the use of company confidential information. Each of these provisions, if desired, will need to be customized for the particular venture, including the enforceability and limitations applicable under state law.

T. NONCIRCUMVENTION

Many buy–sell agreements will contain a "non-circumvention" provision indicating that (1) if and to the extent a factual circumstance should arise that is not expressly provided for in the agreement, the rules applicable to the most analogous situation shall be applied, and (2) each party agrees to avoid conduct that has the purpose or effect of circumventing both the letter and the spirit of the buy–sell agreement. These types of provisions may be important to guard against changes of circumstances that may not have been apparent at the outset of the closely held corporation's existence.

U. TAX DISTINCTIONS BETWEEN C CORPORATIONS AND S CORPORATIONS

As noted above, this *Guidebook* does not detail federal, state, and local tax implications for closely held corporations. However, in drafting a buy–sell agreement, it is important to understand the material distinctions between the tax rules for C corporations versus S corporations. This includes, for instance, the category of shareholders permitted in an S corporation, the tax basis in the shares, and other tax issues that may be implicated.

V. THE RISK OF RELYING ON FORMS

In all areas of contract drafting, and particularly in the case of buy–sell agreements, one is cautioned against relying upon forms. Although a form may be a useful guide as to issues to be addressed and, in certain cases, may provide sample language, the utilization of a form can be problematic. It will not always be obvious from any particular form what was the factual background against which the form was crafted. Also, the drafter needs to take account of underlying state law in drafting a buy–sell agreement; different states, either by statute or case law, have imposed differing limitations upon the acceptable terms of buy–sell agreements. It is important to understand the factual circumstances of the corporation at issue and the nature of its shareholders to draft the agreement that is appropriate for them.

CHAPTER

7 Raising Money, Issuing Shares, and Distributing Assets

A. FINANCING THE CORPORATION THROUGH THE SALE OF STOCK

One of the most important roles of the board of directors is to authorize financing of the corporation to meet its business needs. For many closely held corporations, the business is primarily funded from operating income or some combination of operating income, sales of the corporation's stock to third parties, or debt financing such as borrowing from a bank, shareholders, or others. For other closely held corporations, especially those operating new or expanding early-stage and high-growth businesses, equity financing may clearly be a necessity.

It is the board's responsibility to determine the type and mix of financing that may be suitable for the corporation, as well as the best capital structure (mix of equity and debt). There are also strategic and practical considerations as discussed further below in making these determinations, including the amount of capital needed, the industry in which the corporation operates, and the current economic climate. The board should understand that, in addition to these strategic and practical concerns, raising equity capital by selling the corporation's stock also involves legal compliance concerns, both under state corporation statutes and under federal and state securities laws.

1. Different Types of Equity Investors

Among the most important strategic and practical considerations is determining who will own the corporation's equity. A corporation may want to restrict share ownership to a relatively small group (e.g., family members or active participants in the business) or open investment to financial or outside investors. The decision on share ownership is often inextricably tied to the corporation's long-term strategy, the amount of ownership, and degree of control of the corporation that the current shareholders are willing to surrender in exchange for funding and the extent to which the corporation may benefit from a professional investor or strategic investment partner. Unlike typical debt financing where the relationship is transactional and involves the obligation to pay back the principal with interest, financing through equity involves a long-term relationship with an investor that has an interest—and legal right—in the involvement and success of the corporation's business.

a. *Friends and Family*

The most common type of equity financing, particularly for early-stage companies, is from family members and friends of the founding shareholders. The advantage of this type of financing is that it is much easier and faster to obtain than bank debt or even other sources of equity financing. These friends and family generally are investing in the person rather than the specific business plan and are unlikely to negotiate the terms of the investment or seek an active role within the management of the corporation.

There are downsides to financing through friends and family, however. Selling shares to unsophisticated or nonprofessional investors, even if they are family, friends, or employees of the business, may risk damaging personal relationships if there is a misunderstanding of expectations of the investor's role or the likely success of the corporation in the future. Many of these investors may not fully appreciate the lack of liquidity in the investment. Moreover, in some instances, the decision to sell shares to unsophisticated investors may complicate and sometimes even preclude the later participation of venture capital or other professional investors. The corporation should consult legal counsel with respect to any friends and family financing to minimize these future complications and to ensure compliance with federal and state securities laws, including those applicable to investor qualifications.

b. *Professional Investors and Strategic Partners*

Businesses most suited for equity funding from professional investors, such as "angel" and venture capital investors, are typically high-growth businesses that have the potential to expand in a relatively short number of years. This is because financial or outside investors may have little interest in investing in a minority interest in the nonliquid equity of a closely held corporation if its strategy does not include some means by which investors may eventually realize the value of their investment. To attract such investors, the corporation may be pressed to present evidence of a viable exit strategy within a reasonable time frame, such as an initial public offering or a sale of the corporation.

Selling shares to professional investors may provide a strategic advantage and substantial value to the corporation, in addition to their cash investment, by broadening the experience, expertise, and contacts of its shareholders. Angel investors are typically individual investors who can provide smaller amounts of capital when the early-stage business may not have the demonstrable growth other professional investors would require. The angel investor generally provides more strategic expertise to the corporation than friends and family and typically does not expect an active role in the business.

A venture capital fund is a type of investment vehicle that invests, usually at higher levels than the angel investors and for equity, in early-stage companies that offer a high return potential. Another advantage of financing through a venture fund is that these funds typically set aside substantial reserves to allow them to invest in subsequent rounds of financing should the corporation require additional funds. In addition, managers of venture funds may bring expertise and experience to the corporation in terms of business strategy and management talent and provide valuable business connections.

A corporation with a more established business model and operating history may benefit from funding from a strategic partner. Strategic funding acts like venture capital in that it is usually an equity sale (and not a loan) to another participant in the corporation's industry or an industry with an interest in the corporation's business. Partner financing may be a good alternative for equity financing if the partner is a large business, in the same or similar industry and with relevant customers, salespeople, and marketing capabilities that can be immediately beneficial to the corporation. The strategic investor funds the corporation's growth in exchange for special access to its products, platform, distribution rights (or a combination of these attributes) in addition to its ownership interest, and perhaps even the right to purchase the corporation in the future.

When considering selling shares to venture funds and strategic partners, it is important to understand that these investors typically insist on much tougher financial and governance terms than family and friends and even angel investors (e.g., lower corporate valuations that result in the investor acquiring a larger percentage of the corporation's equity, board representation, or extensive veto powers).

c. Internet-Based Funding from Large Number of Investors

Crowdfunding is a method of raising debt or equity capital through the collective effort of friends, family, customers, and individual investors. Using an online platform, the corporation has the ability to leverage various social networks for greater reach and exposure by pooling small investments from several investors instead of seeking a single investment source. There are a variety of crowdfunding types, including debt-based, rewards-based, and equity crowdfunding. Debt-based crowdfunding is essentially peer-to-peer lending, and rewards-based crowdfunding involves a contribution from an individual to the corporation in exchange for a "reward" (typically a form of the product or service the corporation offers). Equity crowdfunding results in the sale of securities to new shareholders and allows the corporation to control the type of shares it wants to sell, the price of the shares, the valuation of the corporation, and the total amount of capital it wishes to raise. But, having a large number of investors can make subsequent transactions, capital raises, and shareholder voting significantly more challenging for the corporation. Whether crowdfunding is suitable to the corporation depends on the corporation's long-term strategy as well as the type of product or service the corporation offers.

Finally, because crowdfunding may involve a securities offering, the corporation should consult with legal counsel experienced with state corporation law and federal and state securities laws before raising capital this way. These topics are discussed further below.

2. Corporation Law Concerns

The board of directors must authorize and approve the corporation's issuance of securities (either equity or debt) as well as the grant of rights to purchase stock and other securities (e.g., options and warrants). The maximum number of shares a corporation may issue and have outstanding at any one time is limited to the number of authorized shares provided for in the corporation's articles of incorporation. A corporation may increase or decrease the number of authorized shares by amending its articles of incorporation. Amending the articles of incorporation generally requires both board and shareholder approval.

The corporation may prescribe in its articles of incorporation the type of equity it is authorized to issue. If the corporation fails to create different classes of shares, all of the corporation's shares will be regarded as common stock. If the corporation wants all shareholders to have the same rights with respect to voting, dividends, and receipt of the corporation's assets upon liquidation, then the corporation should issue only common stock. However, the corporation may vary the rights of its shareholders by authorizing more than one class of common stock (e.g., Class A, Class B) and authorizing other classes of stock such as preferred stock. In doing so, the corporation generally assigns to each type or class of stock it creates specific rights or limitations with respect to these and other matters. Professional and sophisticated investors often require that they receive preferred stock that sets forth these additional rights in exchange for its capital or even convertible preferred stock that provides for these additional rights plus the ability for the investor to convert its preferred stock into common stock at a specified exchange ratio in the future. The articles of incorporation may also empower the board to tailor such rights and limitations to the needs of the corporation at the time the board authorizes the actual issuance of such shares. In such cases, the shares are frequently referred to as "blank check" shares because the rights and limitations must await the board's passage of a resolution setting forth the particular rights and limitations of those shares.

When issuing shares, the board must determine what consideration or payment the corporation is to receive for such shares. The Model Act and most state corporation statutes permit issuance of stock in consideration of any tangible or intangible property or benefit to the corporation, including cash, promissory notes, services performed, contracts for services to be performed, or other securities of the corporation. Some state corporation statutes (such as California), however, are more restrictive and limit share issuances for certain categories of consideration, especially promissory notes and the promise to perform services in the future. If the corporation is to receive, as consideration for its shares, property or intangible benefits the value of which is uncertain, the Model Act and most state corporation statutes provide that directors must make a determination of the value of the property or intangible benefits.

The issuance of shares must also take into account the rights of existing shareholders. For instance, existing shareholders may have preemptive rights, which are the statutory rights of existing shareholders to avoid dilution of their equity participation and voting power by purchasing a pro rata portion of any new shares being offered. Almost all state corporation statutes provide for preemptive rights, but, under most statutes, shareholders have such rights only if the corporation affirmatively opts in to such right in its articles of incorporation. Under other statutes, shareholders have preemptive rights unless the articles of incorporation opt out. Generally, statutory preemptive rights are difficult to deal with and can restrict and encumber the board in pursuing its financing strategies. On the other hand, in many closely held corporations, the ability of shareholders to maintain their percentage ownership interests can be very important. See chapter 5 for a discussion of preemptive rights.

Shareholder agreements and other agreements to which the corporation is a party (e.g., loan agreements or joint venture agreements) and some special government regulations (e.g., those governing professional service corporations, public utilities, or financial institutions) may contain limitations and restrictions on, or consequences to be incurred by, the corporation as a result of issuing additional shares. See chapter 5 for a discussion of shareholder agreements.

3. Securities Law Concerns

Federal securities laws prohibit the offer and sale of any security without first registering the securities with the SEC and delivering a prospectus containing required information, unless the security or the type of transaction is exempt from registration under federal law. Even if the offering is exempt from registration under federal law, there are state securities laws that may require registration. Federal and state securities laws also impose antifraud liability for misstatements or omissions of material fact in connection with the purchase or sale of any security—even if the offering is exempt from registration at either the state or federal level.

Failure to comply with federal and state securities laws can result in the investor having an absolute right to rescind the transaction (i.e., return the security to the corporation in exchange for return of the purchase price plus interest at a statutory rate) or collect damages for fraud by the corporation and possibly its directors and officers. Such failure to comply or antifraud violations can also result in the corporation and its officers and directors being subject to civil enforcement actions, private claims for money damages, or even criminal prosecution.

It is important to seek legal advice any time that the board is contemplating the offer or sale of stock or other corporate securities and before the offers and sales are made. All offers and sales are subject to federal and state securities laws, including initial issuances to founders as well as offers and sales to employees and to outsiders. Legal counsel can help the board structure a proposed financing or other transaction to come within an available exemption from the federal and applicable state securities law registration requirements and can help the board ensure that disclosures made to investors are adequate to avoid antifraud liability.

Once offers and sales are made, it may be impossible to use an exemption for further sales that would have otherwise been available with advance planning. Mistakes may be extremely costly to the corporation and may not only have an impact on the immediate transaction but also severely limit the corporation's flexibility in obtaining financing in the future.

B. DIVIDENDS AND STOCK REDEMPTIONS

The board of directors has the authority to authorize the corporation to pay dividends or otherwise distribute corporate assets to shareholders. Similarly, when a corporation redeems its stock from existing shareholders, it is another method (besides paying dividends) to return capital to shareholders. The Model Act and most state corporation statutes define "distribution" broadly to include transfers of cash and other property to a shareholder in respect of the corporation's shares, such as payments by a corporation to redeem its own shares. State corporation statutes specify the circumstances under which a corporation may pay a dividend or distribute its assets. The corporation's articles of incorporation or bylaws or other contractual arrangements, such as shareholder agreements or credit agreements, may also contain restrictions or limitations on dividend or other distributions. These restrictions are designed to protect creditors of the corporation who are ultimately entitled to payment prior to return of capital to shareholders. They are also designed to protect shareholders from having corporate assets depleted beyond the point necessary for continuation of corporate business or prevent certain shareholders from receiving a return of capital in preference to other shareholders. Directors who permit the payment of dividends or the distribution of assets in contravention of relevant restrictions and limitations may expose themselves to personal liability.

1. Strategic and Practical Concerns

So long as the corporation is not restricted by the statutory and contractual requirements discussed above, deciding when to pay a dividend, how much the dividend should be, and what form it should take (i.e., cash, stock, or other property) is left to the discretion of the board of directors. Because dividends represent a transfer of assets from the corporation to its shareholders, directors should consider how that transfer may affect the corporation's ability to realize its short-term and long-term strategic goals.

Shareholders in a corporation rarely have the same economic standing and level of financial security. Consequently, some shareholders may view and come to rely upon dividends as a source of short-term cash flow. Others, however, may be more interested in the corporation reinvesting earnings as a means of increasing the long-term value of their shares. Frequently, the dividend policy adopted by the board will seek to address both concerns by distributing some but not all of the corporation's earnings. In many closely held corporations, the distribution policy may well be a subject set forth in a shareholder agreement (see discussion of tax concerns in subsection 3 of this chapter).

If the corporation has elected S corporation tax status, the board should consider adopting a dividend policy that, at the very least, will distribute to the shareholders enough money to meet their periodic tax obligations incurred as a result of their stock ownership. Corporations typically adopt a formula to determine the highest possible tax rate incurred by any particular shareholder so that no shareholder will receive less than the taxes such shareholder incurs.

Equally important as the amount of the dividend is the timing of the dividend payments. Boards should take into consideration the timing of the tax payments required of shareholders, as well as the corporation's own contractual obligations and cash flow needs, in establishing the schedule upon which dividends will be paid. Many corporations pay dividends on an annual basis after fiscal year results have been tabulated and reserves established for the following fiscal year. Others declare and pay dividends on a quarterly or semiannual basis. For many closely held S corporations, dividends typically are made quarterly to coincide with the shareholders' quarterly tax payments.

2. Corporation Law Concerns

Restrictions on distributions to shareholders vary significantly from one corporation statute to the next. Most restrict the payment of dividends or the distribution of assets if such payment or distribution would render the corporation insolvent. The Model Act and most state corporation statutes prohibit a corporation from paying dividends or distributing assets if, after giving effect to such action, the corporation would not be able to pay its debts as they become due in the usual course of business, or the corporation's total assets would be less than the sum of its total liabilities plus (unless the articles of incorporation permit otherwise) the amount that would be needed, if the corporation were to be dissolved at the time of the distribution, to satisfy the preferential rights upon dissolution of shareholders whose preferential rights are superior to those receiving the distribution.

Directors may be personally liable for wrongful payment of dividends or distribution of assets. As a result, boards of struggling companies often obtain a solvency opinion from an independent financial advisor before authorizing dividends or other distributions to shareholders.

If the primary purpose of the payment of dividends or the distribution of corporate assets to its shareholders is to frustrate the collection efforts of legitimate creditors of the corporation, the distributions may be nullified as fraudulent conveyances or recovered as a preference in a bankruptcy proceeding. If the corporation has engaged in a fraudulent conveyance, the assets must be returned to the corporation.

3. Other Distribution Issues

Whether a corporation pays a dividend to its shareholders or redeems its shareholders' shares may have a different tax consequence for those shareholders. In addition, the payment of dividends in a closely held corporation may be confused with the payment of compensation for services performed. This confusion most often arises when some or all of the shareholders are employees of the corporation. The board should set a dividend policy in which all shareholders are treated alike and separately consider and set the compensation for those shareholders who are also employees. Failing to distinguish between what is a dividend and what is compensation can have significant legal as well as tax implications and can raise concerns for nonemployee shareholders about fair treatment.

C. GIVING EMPLOYEES AN OWNERSHIP INTEREST

Giving employees an ownership interest in the corporation is common. From the point of view of the corporation, stock-based compensation may permit a business to attract and retain key employees while conserving cash. Making employees owners may also create incentive to work for long-term enhancement of the corporation's value by giving them a share of the future upside and the potential for long-term capital gains tax treatment.

There are, however, important practical and legal issues raised by offering stock to employees (in addition to the corporate and securities law issues discussed above with respect to any stock issuance). First, closely held corporations have no public market for their shares and stock-based compensation is illiquid. Second, the employee may be taxed at the time of receipt of the stock under certain circumstances. Third, those employees acquiring stock gain legal rights (e.g., rights to inspect corporate records and to receive notice of and attend and vote at shareholder meetings) and standing to challenge or question board decisions by legal action and otherwise. As a result, the corporation may have to adopt more formal procedures than what existed when all the shares were held by a relatively few shareholders, and corporate action may become more complex, contentious, and time-consuming.

1. Stock

If the corporation decides to issue shares to its employees, it should require them to enter into appropriate buy–sell agreements providing for redemption of the shares by the corporation in the event of death or termination of employment or in the event the employee desires to sell the shares to a third party (see discussion of such buy–sell agreements in chapter 6). In addition, the corporation should consider imposing a vesting schedule with respect to the shares it issues to its employees to ensure those employees continue to work for the corporation for some period of time in the future to contribute to its success. This type of stock is sometimes referred to as restricted stock. If the employee with restricted stock leaves the corporation for any reason, the corporation usually has the right to redeem the unvested stock from the employee at a lower price as compared to the price of vested stock.

Similar to stock options discussed below, there are tax, securities, and accounting issues for both the corporation and the recipient of the restricted stock to consider before issuing restricted stock.

2. Stock Options

Instead of issuing stock to its employees, corporations may instead use options to acquire shares of stock to provide employees with equity incentive compensation. A stock option gives the holder of the option the right over a defined period of time to purchase a defined number of shares of stock of the corporation at a predetermined purchase price. The benefit to the employee of receiving a stock option rather than shares of stock outright is that it provides the employee with the opportunity to participate in the growth of the corporation without having to immediately pay for the shares or the corresponding tax liability. But this value will only be obtained when and if the option holder exercises the right to purchase the shares and ultimately become a shareholder.

The same considerations that apply to issuance of stock to employees apply to stock option grants. In addition, the tax, securities, and accounting rules associated with the granting and exercise of stock options are complex. Determination of fair market value, essential for granting certain tax-advantaged options, poses difficulties due to the absence of a trading market. Employees and the closely held corporation can be adversely affected by tax, accounting, and other rules relating to options if careful planning is not undertaken when establishing a stock option plan and granting options.

3. Phantom Stock

An alternative to issuance of shares or the grant of options to buy shares is for the corporation to issue quasi-equity inducements, such as "phantom" stock, that reward employees financially for increases in the value of the corporation without giving them an ownership interest. Phantom stock and similar compensatory rewards can be thought of as deferred bonus arrangements that entitle an employee to receive cash in an amount equal to the increase in value of stock between the grant date and a later specified date (e.g., termination of employment, sale of the corporation, or commencement of an initial public offering). Phantom stock and similar bonus units may be made subject to vesting requirements. They may also provide for the payment of the appreciated value over a period of time to avoid draining the corporation of cash.

4. Employee Stock Ownership Plan

One of the most difficult problems for owners of closely held corporations is a succession plan that allows the owner to monetize the value created in the corporation for retirement or other purposes. Some business owners want to transition the corporation to a family member or sell to a third party. However, a management buyout by a family member may be difficult to achieve if the corporation has significantly appreciated in value, and a third-party sale transaction would risk limiting the family's influence over the future operations of the corporation and the ongoing treatment of the corporation's employees. In this situation, the owner may consider an employee stock ownership plan (ESOP) as a succession planning tool that involves the sale of the corporation to a retirement trust established for the benefit of the corporation's employees.

A corporation considering an ESOP should consult with an experienced ESOP advisor to assess its feasibility for the particular corporation, ensure compliance with federal employment compensation rules under the Employee Retirement Income Security Act of 1974, and consider applicable tax implications.

CHAPTER

8 Merger, Sale of Assets, and Change of Entity

A merger or asset sale is often used to sell a business, although mergers can also be used to recapitalize a corporation, create a holding company structure, or acquire other entities. A corporation also may change its form of entity by converting from a corporation into a different legal entity, such as a limited liability company, or change its state of incorporation from one state to another through a domestication. Each of these transactions is subject to state corporation law requirements, which specify required shareholder and director approvals as well as certain transaction terms that must be set forth in a written plan describing the transaction. Apart from asset sales, these transactions also require one or more state filings with the applicable secretary of state or similar governmental authority to become effective.

The requirements applicable to these transactions vary state to state, including shareholder approval requirements and the availability of appraisal rights to dissenting shareholders. These transactions must also comply with the corporation's articles of incorporation and bylaws as well as any shareholder agreements in effect. See discussion of shareholder agreements, including buy–sell agreements, in chapters 5 and 6. Corporations should consult with tax and legal advisors experienced with these types of transactions before the corporation enters into any agreement to merge, sell its assets, or engage in other similar transaction.

A. MERGERS

A merger is a transaction in which two or more entities merge into a single entity, which is sometimes referred to as the "survivor." Although mergers are used most often to sell a corporation, they can also be used in recapitalizations and internal restructurings, such as forming a holding company structure. In a merger transaction, where the non-surviving corporation's shareholders receive cash or other property and have no continuing interest in the surviving corporation, the merger effectively has the same result as selling all of the outstanding equity of the corporation.

When a typical merger becomes effective, the first entity ceases to exist and the survivor continues its legal existence. One of the most important aspects of a merger is that the survivor succeeds by operation of law to all of the non-surviving entity's rights, assets, properties, and liabilities. For example, if the non-surviving entity owned real estate or owed a financial obligation to a creditor, the surviving entity after the merger automatically becomes the owner of that real estate and assumes that financial obligation.

Under state corporation statutes, the terms of a merger must be set forth in a plan of merger or an agreement and plan of merger. Among other things, the plan or agreement must specify which entity is the survivor and what happens to the outstanding equity interests of the non-surviving corporation. For example, in a merger transaction, the plan or agreement will specify the consideration payable to selling corporation's shareholders once their shares are canceled in the merger. Although a plan of merger can be straightforward and contain only the information required by the applicable state corporation statute, an agreement and plan of merger can be a much longer and more complex document that contains numerous representations and warranties as to the corporation's business, covenants related to operations prior to effecting the transaction, conditions to the merger being finalized, and indemnification obligations if the representations and warranties are not accurate or the covenants are not performed. An agreement and plan of merger is typically used in a negotiated transaction between two unaffiliated parties. However, in order to avoid having the negotiated provisions set forth in the public filing with the applicable state, the parties may prepare and file a separate plan of merger that contains only the abbreviated information required by the applicable corporation statute.

Under state corporation statutes, the plan of merger or agreement and plan of merger must be approved by the board of directors and, subject to certain exceptions, the shareholders. When shareholder approval is required, the board of directors typically must issue its recommendation that shareholders vote in favor of the merger. Most mergers must be approved by a majority of the corporation's shareholders. As explained below, the ability of a majority of the shareholders to bind all of the shareholders is usually an important reason for structuring a corporate sale as a merger rather than a stock sale. The required shareholder vote, however, will depend on state law and the corporation's articles of incorporation and bylaws. Particularly among closely held corporations, a corporation's organizational documents or a shareholder agreement may require a supermajority vote or even unanimous shareholder approval or approval by certain classes of shares to authorize a merger.

In substance, the sale of a corporation through a merger has the same result as a stock purchase; it transfers equity ownership of the corporation from its shareholders to the buyer. A stock transfer, however, requires each shareholder to transfer their shares to the buyer. For many corporations, having each shareholder sign a purchase agreement presents logistical challenges. It may also allow a single shareholder to block the sale of the corporation if the buyer insists on obtaining 100 percent ownership, which is usually the case. Mergers, therefore, are typically used when the number of shareholders makes it difficult or impractical to obtain unanimous shareholder participation in a stock transfer. This assumes, however, that a majority of the shareholders approve the merger under the applicable state corporation statute and the corporation's organizational documents and that a higher shareholder approval threshold is not required.

To protect nonconsenting shareholders, state corporation statutes usually give those shareholders the right to dissent from a merger and exercise appraisal rights. In that case, the dissenting shareholders forgo the merger consideration and instead become entitled to have a court determine the "fair value" of their shares. To perfect their appraisal rights, dissenting shareholders must usually notify the corporation of their intent to seek appraisal and not vote in favor of the merger. State corporation statutes generally require strict compliance with the procedures contained in the appraisal statutes, which vary state to state.

Corporations should review the terms of any shareholder agreements or buy–sell agreements before proceeding with a merger. These agreements are discussed in greater detail in chapters 5 and 6. For example, a shareholder agreement or buy–sell agreement may specify the required vote for a merger, contain voting agreements among the shareholders, waive appraisal rights, trigger rights of first refusal, or contain "drag-along" rights that require shareholders to support a sale transaction. The duties of directors in a merger context are discussed in chapter 3.

B. SALE OF ASSETS

Although corporations often engage in a variety of sales of assets, significant asset dispositions involving a sale of substantially all the assets outside the regular course of business are governed by state corporation statutes. Such transactions can fundamentally change a shareholder's investment in the corporation. For example, a corporation can effectively sell its business through an asset sale rather than a merger or a sale of the corporation's stock.

State corporation statutes vary, but an asset disposition consisting of all or substantially all of the corporation's assets or, under the Model Act, that leaves the corporation without a "significant continuing business activity" must be approved by the board of directors and the shareholders. The required shareholder vote is usually a majority of the outstanding shares, but the applicable state corporation statute or the corporation's articles of incorporation, bylaws, or shareholder agreement may establish a different threshold.

It may not always be clear whether shareholder approval is required when a corporation sells its assets but retains some of its assets or a small continuing business activity. Some states, including Delaware, apply both quantitative and qualitative tests to determine whether the asset disposition constitutes "all or substantially all" of the corporation's assets. Other states have enacted safe harbors to help clarify when shareholder approval is not required. Under the Model Act, for example, a corporation is conclusively deemed to have retained a significant continuing business activity (and, therefore, shareholder approval is not required) if it retains a business activity that represents at least (1) 25 percent of its total assets at the end of the most recently completed fiscal year, and (2) 25 percent of either income from continuing operations before taxes or 25 percent of revenues from continuing operations, in each case for the most recently completed fiscal year.

Asset sales are often favored by buyers because (1) the parties can pick and choose which assets the buyer will acquire, (2) the buyer typically does not assume any of the selling corporation's liabilities absent express agreement, and (3) the buyer obtains a "step-up" in tax basis in the acquired assets (meaning that the price paid for the assets is the buyer's new tax basis).

One downside to asset sales is that the seller's contracts and permits may not be freely assignable to the buyer. Many contracts require the counterparty's consent before they can be assigned to someone else. For example, the buyer may agree to assume a real estate lease from the seller, but that lease may require the landlord's consent before it can be assigned. From the selling corporation's perspective, another downside to an asset sale is that, if the selling corporation is not retaining an ongoing business activity, it will have to wind up and liquidate its business before distributing all of its cash or other assets to shareholders. Depending on the complexity of the selling corporation's business, the wind-up and liquidation process can be time-consuming and may require the corporation to set aside a portion of the sale proceeds to satisfy its creditors and contingent liabilities.

Asset sales may result in greater tax liability for the corporation or its shareholders when compared to a merger or sale of stock. Depending on the nature of the corporation's retained liabilities, the liquidation process can be cumbersome and delay distributions to shareholders. In addition, sellers should be aware of fraudulent conveyance laws, which protect creditors from transactions designed to avoid their claims. Finally, as with mergers, corporations must review closely their articles of incorporation, bylaws, and any shareholder agreements to determine whether they impose additional requirements on asset sales.

C. CHANGE OF ENTITY OR STATE OF ORGANIZATION

Under most state corporation statutes, a corporation may change into a different entity through a transaction known as a "conversion." For example, a corporation may convert into a limited liability company or limited partnership. Similarly, most states allow other business entities to convert into corporations. There are numerous reasons why an entity might convert into a different type of entity, including tax, corporate governance, and attracting new investors who prefer a particular entity type.

Under state corporation statutes that provide for conversions, the terms of a conversion must be set forth in a plan of conversion. The plan must include the terms providing for the reclassification of the corporation's shares into equity interests of the new entity (e.g., converting each share of common stock into a corresponding unit or membership interest of the new limited liability company). The plan of conversion must be approved by the board of directors and the shareholders. Usually, a majority of the shareholders must approve the conversion, but the applicable state corporation statute or the corporation's articles of incorporation, bylaws, or shareholder agreement may establish a different threshold.

From a legal perspective, the converting entity's existence continues without interruption even though it has become a different legal entity. The resulting entity succeeds to all the converting entity's rights, assets, obligations, and liabilities. The corporation should review its contracts and permits, however, to see whether they impose restrictions on conversions.

Many states also permit a corporation to change its governing law through what is commonly known as a "domestication." For example, a Florida corporation could domesticate and become a Delaware corporation. In a domestication, the corporation continues its legal existence uninterrupted. Similar to a conversion, state corporation statutes require the corporation to adopt a "plan of domestication," which must be approved by the board of directors and the shareholders. Importantly, the domestication transaction must also be permitted by the laws of the state into which the corporation intends to domesticate.

CHAPTER

9 Director, Officer, and Shareholder Liability Concerns

A. OVERVIEW

Directors, officers, and shareholders of a closely held business can face liability to third parties and/or to the corporation itself. In order to attract and retain top-quality managers, consideration should be given to what has been referred to as the "three-legged stool" of protection: (1) exculpation from liability in the first instance, (2) end-of-the-matter indemnification against liability (to the extent permitted by statute and public policy) and advancement of legal defense expenses, and (3) access to adequate director and officer liability insurance coverage, where the business entity cannot or will not provide advancement or indemnification.

B. DIRECTOR AND OFFICER LIABILITY

Directors and officers may incur personal liability for breaches of either their duty of care or duty of loyalty (which typically includes a duty to act in good faith) or for failure to meet the requirements of certain other applicable laws.

1. State Law Liability

Directors and officers may be liable for money damages for breach of their duty of care or duty of loyalty in actions brought by or on behalf of the corporation or in direct actions by shareholders. State corporation statutes also contain special provisions making directors liable for payment of illegal dividends or other distributions. See chapter 3 for a discussion of these duties and chapter 7 for a discussion of statutory requirements prior to the issuance of dividends and other distributions.

2. Liability under Other Laws

Directors and officers can be personally liable under the federal and state securities laws, in some cases even where they act in good faith. Directors and officers also may be subject to personal liability under other state and federal statutes such as environmental laws and employee federal income tax withholding provisions. Timely legal advice and careful monitoring of management programs directed toward corporate legal compliance should provide substantial safeguards against personal liability.

C. SHAREHOLDER LIABILITY—PIERCING THE CORPORATE VEIL

Although a shareholder of a corporation is generally not liable for the obligations of the corporation, under limited circumstances courts will disregard the existence of the corporate form and impose personal liability on shareholders for obligations of the corporation. Courts call this "piercing the corporate veil." The willingness of courts to disregard the corporate form varies from state to state. The rationale often employed by the courts for piercing the corporate veil is that the corporation has been managed in ways that ignore, or are inconsistent with, the concept of the corporation as a separate entity. The doctrine of piercing the corporate veil generally is only successful against shareholders of corporations that are closely held. Consequently, directors of closely held corporations should be aware of the possible consequences of lax management practices and should seek to avoid conditions that might expose shareholders to personal liability. A number of important factors have been cited as justification for piercing the corporate veil in those cases that have resulted in shareholder liability. These factors include the following.

1. Inadequate Capitalization from Inception

One of the reasons cited by courts for piercing the corporate veil is that the corporation never received adequate capital to operate the business and provide for the foreseeable obligations and risks inherent in the business. In a tort case, for example, where the plaintiff is injured in an accident involving a corporate vehicle and the corporation does not have adequate insurance coverage, undercapitalization from inception might be sufficient for a court to justify piercing.

2. Fraud or Misrepresentation

In a contract case, where a party has voluntarily chosen to enter into the contract with the corporation, courts typically require that some element of deception or inequity be involved to justify piercing the veil. Misrepresenting the finances of the corporation or otherwise misleading the other party to the contract could supply the necessary element.

3. Commingling Corporate and Shareholder Assets; Siphoning Off Assets

Courts have also cited indiscriminate use of corporate funds or other assets for shareholder personal, nonbusiness purposes, or withdrawing funds needed for corporate operations, as factors in support of piercing.

4. Inattention to Corporate Formalities

Failure to observe corporate formalities is one of the most frequently cited factors justifying disregard of the corporate form. Failure to adopt bylaws, hold annual meetings and keep minutes, and maintain books and records are factors that have been noted to support piercing the corporate veil.

D. EXCULPATION FROM LIABILITY FOR MONEY DAMAGES

The Model Act and most state corporation statutes permit the corporation to eliminate or limit the liability of directors to the corporation or its shareholders for money damages for breaches of certain duties, most frequently the duty of care. For instance, the Model Act permits inclusion of a provision in the articles of incorporation eliminating or limiting a director's personal liability for money damages, except liability for the receipt of a financial benefit to which the director is not entitled, the intentional infliction of harm on the corporation, an unlawful distribution, or an intentional violation of criminal law. The director is only exculpated from liability for conduct as a director and in most states, no such exculpation will apply to conduct as an officer (although some states, including Delaware, have modified their corporation statutes to allow officers to be exculpated from liability as well). Even as to conduct as a director, the exculpation will only apply to liability for the payment of money damages and will not shield the director from injunctive relief (i.e., being ordered by a court to take certain actions or not take certain actions). Finally, exculpation provisions typically must be included in the articles of incorporation, not the bylaws.

Shareholders in a closely held corporation may also enter into an agreement pursuant to which the duties of all or certain directors are delegated to others. To be effective, all shareholders must sign such an agreement. The Model Act provides that an agreement authorized by shareholders that restricts the discretion or powers of a director relieves that director from liability otherwise imposed by law. See discussion of such unanimous shareholder agreements in chapter 5.

E. INDEMNIFICATION

State corporation statutes specify the circumstances in which the corporation is permitted or required to indemnify its directors and officers against liability and related reasonable expenses incurred in connection with their service to the corporation. Under the Model Act, a director or officer may be indemnified for liabilities and expenses only if the director or officer took the actions giving rise to the claim in good faith and with a reasonable belief that their conduct was in the best interests of the corporation. In the case of criminal proceedings, the director or officer must also have had no reasonable cause to believe that their conduct was unlawful. Under the Model Act and many state corporation statutes, corporations have the power to indemnify directors and officers in actions by third parties, including class actions, for expenses (including attorneys' fees), judgments, fines, and amounts paid in settlement of the actions. In derivative actions brought in the name of the corporation itself, indemnification of the director or officer is allowed only for expenses (including attorneys' fees), but when a person has been found liable, indemnification is allowed only with court approval. Further, the Model Act provides that amounts paid in settlement of a derivative action may be indemnified only if approved by a court. This approach—permitting indemnification in derivative actions for amounts awarded as a judgment or amounts paid in settlement—is contrary to the corporation law in certain states (including Delaware), where public policy prevents such payments as "circular" (i.e., the corporation paying itself); in such states, however, public policy may allow for indemnification through director and officer liability insurance (see section F).

The Model Act provides that indemnification for reasonable expenses (including court costs and legal fees) is mandatory if the director or officer has been "wholly successful" in the defense of any action, on the merits or otherwise.

The Model Act and most state corporation statutes permit, and many corporations have provisions in their articles of incorporation or bylaws mandating, indemnification to the fullest extent permitted by law. Such broad, mandatory indemnification may be undesirable from the corporation's perspective—especially to the extent that it binds the corporation to indemnify not only directors and officers but also other employees and agents of the corporation.

Mandatory indemnification provisions in the articles of incorporation or bylaws should be reviewed carefully on a "clear day," namely, when there is no dispute pending. Corporations may also have separate indemnification contracts with directors and officers to provide mandatory indemnification to the extent that the applicable statute permits. From the perspective of the director or officer, the main advantages of indemnification contracts are that they may not be rescinded without their consent (whereas an articles or bylaw indemnification provision may be subject to amendment) and that they may provide more advantageous terms than under the articles or bylaws for advancing expenses and indemnification procedures and timing.

Directors and officers should be aware that a corporation's ability to honor its indemnification obligations is only as strong as the corporation's financial condition. If the corporation is in financial distress, relying upon the corporation's pledge of indemnification could leave the director or officer with personal liability, unless insurance or other indemnity is available. And, in the context of the bankruptcy of the corporation, the issue can arise as to who may claim ownership of the director and officer indemnity insurance policy and its proceeds—the bankruptcy debtor (business) or its directors and officers. Corporations and their directors and officers should seek expert advice in connection with obtaining this insurance as such policies are typically very complex.

F. ADVANCES FOR EXPENSES

The right of a director or officer to indemnification is usually precipitated by the conclusion of the litigation or proceeding after their conduct has been fully adjudicated. However, prior to that point, the indemnified parties, in defending their conduct, will often incur substantial attorneys' fees and other expenses. The Model Act and state corporation statutes generally specify the circumstances in which corporations may advance funds to pay or reimburse reasonable expenses incurred in defense of a matter before final disposition of the proceeding and final determination of the right to indemnification for those expenses.

Governing documents may provide for mandatory advancement of reasonable expenses where the claimant has been made a party to (or is threatened to be made a party to) a covered proceeding by reason of the fact that the person was a director, officer, or other manager and has incurred and will incur defense expenses. However, these expense obligations may be substantial so the decision to provide for mandatory advancement of expenses should be carefully considered.

A demand for advancement typically is accompanied by a written "undertaking," which provides that the claimant will repay amounts advanced if it later is determined that they are not entitled to end-of-the-matter indemnification. If the business entity refuses to provide advancement, the claimant may initiate an enforcement proceeding to seek an award of the amounts to be advanced, prejudgment interest, and "fees-for-fees" (the attorneys' fees and other expenses incurred in preparing and prosecuting the enforcement action). If a claimant refuses to repay amounts advanced at the conclusion of the underlying matter, the business entity may pursue a "clawback" proceeding, for a return of the amounts advanced plus prejudgment interest accruing from the date of each advancement payment.

G. INSURANCE

Generally, state corporation statutes permit corporations to purchase directors and officers liability insurance (commonly referred to as "D&O insurance"). D&O insurance may be used by the corporation to fill gaps in its indemnification coverage. These gaps include situations in which the corporation is not permitted to provide exculpation or indemnification or where the corporation's indemnification obligation exists, but the corporation is unable to meet the financial obligation of indemnification. D&O insurance policies typically have an "insured versus insured" coverage exclusion (i.e., excluding coverage of disputes among the insured, including between the company and its directors and officers, or among the directors/officers themselves); however, such policies typically provide coverage for derivative actions from that exclusion. It is important to negotiate insurance coverage and focus on the policy's definition of a "claim" to avoid an unwelcome declination of coverage.

CHAPTER 10 Corporate Books, Records, and Reporting

The ongoing maintenance by a corporation of its books and records is required by the Model Act and state corporation statutes generally. For closely held corporations, well-organized and complete records may be especially helpful in demonstrating the separateness of the corporate entity and its shareholders, thereby helping to maintain the liability shield of the corporation (see "piercing the corporate veil" discussion in chapter 9). Also, in many commercial or financial transactions, the other party will insist upon evidence of board or shareholder authorization of the transaction. If the corporation anticipates entering into certain significant corporate transactions, such as debt or equity financings or sale of the business, the other party will most likely ask to review all the historical records of the corporation, including the stock register. Thus, the timely and accurate maintenance of corporate records cannot be overemphasized.

A. MINUTES, WRITTEN CONSENTS, ARTICLES OF INCORPORATION, AND BYLAWS

The Model Act and most state corporation statutes require that a corporation keep written minutes of the meetings of its shareholders, board of directors, and committees of the board; copies of actions of the shareholders or the board and committees of the board taken by written consent; an up-to-date copy of the articles of incorporation and bylaws; and any written communication to shareholders in the last three years. The Model Act also requires corporations to maintain all financial statements prepared for the corporation, accounting records that permit preparation of its financial statements and its annual reports filed with the Secretary of State. State corporation statutes vary on the length of time the required records should be maintained. The statutes do not specify the amount of detail to be included in board or shareholder minutes, and it is generally advisable to keep the minutes concise, but accurately reflect all actions taken. State corporation statutes often do not specify how the records are to be maintained. A number of state corporation statutes require that the specified records be kept at the corporation's principal place of business, while others do not specify where or how such records should be maintained. The Model Act, for example, states that the required records must be maintained in a manner so that they may be made available for inspection in a reasonable time.

B. FINANCIAL RECORDS AND STATEMENTS

Under state corporation statutes, a corporation is required to maintain current accounting records that are sufficiently complete to permit the preparation of its financial statements. The Model Act and most state corporation statutes do not prescribe standards for the format of accounting records or financial statements to be prepared or maintained. The Model Act requires that the financial statements to be maintained are those that the corporation uses in its business. For many smaller closely held corporations, this may only be annual tax returns. It is important to review the applicable statute carefully as some state corporation statutes have a requirement for preparation of specific financial statements, such as an annual balance sheet and income statement, with some requiring a distribution of such financial statements to shareholders.

C. SHAREHOLDER AND DIRECTOR AND OFFICER RECORDS

In addition to a record of corporate actions and financial information, a corporation must maintain basic information concerning its shareholders and its directors and officers. Generally, a corporation must be able to produce a list of its shareholders showing their addresses and the share class and number of shares owned by each shareholder. The shareholder list is usually derived from the share register maintained by the corporation, which records all issuances, transfers and cancellations of shares, the date each such event occurred, and the certificate number of any share certificates issued. Many state corporation statutes provide that the corporation must also maintain a current list and business address of its officers and directors.

Generally, a corporation may maintain all or part of its books and records in electronic form. The Model Act permits a corporation flexibility in using technology, provided that the method of storage allows for the electronically stored books and records to be produced in written form within a reasonable time.

D. RIGHT TO INSPECT BOOKS AND RECORDS

The Model Act and many state corporation statutes give shareholders, upon prior request, an immediate right to inspect and copy the articles of incorporation and bylaws of the corporation, the minutes of shareholder meetings and any written communication to shareholders made during the previous three years, and the names and business addresses of the directors and officers. Prior to a meeting of shareholders, a shareholder or their agents may also inspect the list of shareholders entitled to vote at the meeting. Generally, this list must be available for inspection at least two days after notice of the meeting is given through the date of the meeting.

Shareholders also may inspect additional books and records of the corporation, but their right to do so is neither absolute nor immediate. If a shareholder can demonstrate a purpose that is made in good faith and relevant to their interest as a shareholder and not simply a disagreement with management, then the shareholder can inspect and copy excerpts of board and committee meeting minutes, accounting records, and shareholder records that are relevant to the shareholder's proper purpose for the request. A corporation may limit or deny a shareholder's access to its books and records if the corporation believes that the shareholder is acting in bad faith or will misappropriate or otherwise use the information in a manner that harms or is intended to harm the corporation.

With proper grounds, a court may order a corporation to open its books and records for inspection. The inspection rights under most state corporation statutes set forth a statutory procedure which provides shareholders, with a proper purpose, the ability to obtain court ordered information about the corporation and to inspect and copy documents which deal with the shareholder's interest in the corporation.

It is not uncommon for financial investors in closely held corporations to negotiate the right to receive more extensive information, including monthly or quarterly financial statements and annual budgets and periodic comparisons to budget. In addition, these investors may also negotiate the right to send observers to board meetings. Although board observers do not have votes at the meeting, they are generally given copies of the information that is distributed to board members before and during the meeting. See chapter 2 for a discussion of board observers.

E. ANNUAL REPORTING

Under the Model Act and most state corporation statutes, a corporation incorporated or doing business in the state is required to file an annual or biannual report with the secretary of state. A corporation may be administratively dissolved or its charter revoked if it fails to file this report.

The content and form of the reports vary widely from state to state. Under the Model Act, the corporation is required to file only limited information: the location of the principal office, the names and addresses of the corporation's directors and principal officers, a general description of the business, and the corporation's capital structure. Typically, the corporation must pay a fee along with the filing.

Index